TRADITIONAL NEEDLE ARTS

NEEDLEPOINT

TRADITIONAL NEEDLE ARTS

NEEDLEPOINT

20 classic projects

ANNA PEARSON

PHOTOGRAPHY BY TIM IMRIE

MITCHELL BEAZLEY

First published in Great Britain in 1997
by Mitchell Beazley, an imprint of
Reed Consumer Books Limited
Michelin House, 81 Fulham Road,
London SW3 6RB
and Auckland, Melbourne, Singapore and Toronto

Editors	JULIA NORTH AND
	MARGOT RICHARDSON
Senior Art Editor	SUSAN DOWNING
Photographic Art Director/	
Stylist	DEENA BEVERLEY
Designer	RUTH PRENTICE
Production	JULIETTE BUTLER
Charts	HELENA & RAYMOND
	TURVEY
Executive Art Editor	JANIS UTTON
Executive Editor	JUDITH MORE
Art Director	GAYE ALLEN

A CIP record for this book is available from the
British Library

ISBN 1 85732 790 X

The publishers have made every effort to ensure
that all instructions given in this book are accurate
and safe but they cannot accept liability for any
resulting injury, damage or loss to either person or
property, whether direct or consequential and
howsoever arising.
The colours in the keys and charts in this book are as
near to the true colour of the yarns as possible, but
some variation may occur. The author and publishers
will be grateful for any information which will assist
them in keeping future editions up to date.

Typeset in Perpetua 12/16 and 10/12pt
Index compiled by Hilary Bird
Produced by Mandarin Offset

Printed and bound in Hong Kong

Contents

Introduction

The history of needlepoint – or "canvas work" as it is called by some purists to distinguish it from the technique of needlepoint lace – goes back a very long way. The advent, in the 16th century, of the tent stitch – a small stitch over a single canvas thread – which is so hard-wearing, means that many pieces have managed to survive until the present day.

Some people incorrectly associate the word tapestry with canvas work. Tapestries are large wall-hangings such as those seen in French châteaux and stately houses, and are woven on a loom. Needlepoint – as it is called in this book – has always been extremely popular in Britain, Europe as a whole, America and Australia. England and France have always loved the fine flower and other pictorial subjects, and enjoyed working elegant chair seats and rugs, as well as cushions and other small items. North America seems to have had a wonderful mix of design sources. Until 1776 and the War of Independence, most needlework supplies were imported from England; after this date, French items became more popular and, in the early 19th century, Berlin woolwork from Germany became fashionable in the United States.

Traditional needlepoint completely covers the canvas with stitching – so while samplers were frequently worked in wool, the earliest examples we can study of domestic needlepoint are cushions and table rugs. Cushions were necessary for comfort. Even a great house in the 16th century would have had only one chair, for the lord of the house; everyone else would have sat on long, hard benches – so in early inventories numerous cushions were listed as

LEFT This delft pottery picture dates back to 1715 and reflects the 18th-century fashion for blue and white Chinese porcelain. Initially these imported items were very expensive, but were soon copied both in Holland and many areas of Britain.

BELOW Present-day stitchers often assume that designs will not be authentic-looking unless they choose very muted shades. This amazing Florentine design, worked in its original colour scheme, shows that bold colours and designs were often favoured by embroiderers of the past.

important items. Early furniture was extremely plain, often made of oak, and so the habit of stitching table carpets to cover drab pieces of furniture found favour.

Until the 16th century, most needlework was undertaken purely for ecclesiastical purposes. However, although Elizabeth I granted a charter to the City of London Broderers' Company in 1561, the organisation is thought to have existed since the 14th century.

Interest in needlework was not confined to England, however. Marie de Medici (1573-1642), the wife of Henry IV of France, was a notable needleworker whose embroidered floral designs were highly influential, and subsequently copied by the ladies of the French court. At Parham Park in Sussex, England, the Great Bed is believed to have been embroidered with silks and enriched by gold thread and pearls by Marie de Medici and needlepointed in Hungarian Point by Mary Queen of Scots.

Later, it was common for many large houses to employ at least one professional male needle-worker to help the ladies design pieces and work on the larger items. The changing fashions in the world of furniture, together with what could be purchased ready-made, obviously played an important part in what was needed in the way of textile decoration.

At about the time of the Restoration of Charles II, in 1660, walnut gained popularity over oak for furniture. It had many advantages, not least of which was its highly decorative nature – especially burr walnut. This is significant because it resulted in a decline of popularity in the covering of tables, and table carpets soon developed into floor rugs. It is interesting to note that in 16th-century portraits there is frequently a table draped with a rug, while in the 17th century the subject stands on the rug. Nothing was ever included in a portrait unless it conveyed the wealth, good taste and culture of the person painted.

Chairs gradually became more comfortable with the arrival of upholstery. Wing chairs appeared toward the end of the 17th century and the early part of the 18th century. There are some magnificent examples to be found in museums and historic houses, still in good condition, both with floral and Florentine needlework.

One of the most interesting aspects of needlepoint that these early pieces highlight is the fine canvas that was frequently used. Today's needleworker often rejects any design on canvas with small holes, yet we have light and magnification possibilities not dreamt of in earlier times. Also, bright colours were popular. Too often, present-day stitchers consider that a piece will not be authentic unless worked in faded shades, whereas you only have to look at the areas of historic pieces that have not been exposed to bright light, or their inside turnings, to be amazed at their extreme boldness of colour.

Hangings for the lord and lady's bed were also a practical, if massive, needlepoint project. Until the end of the 15th century, many houses had no glass in their windows, so bed-hangings were necessary to keep out draughts and also to give privacy, as the bed at that period would not have been in a separate room.

Toward the end of the century, Italian velvets started to be imported and so the fashion for "slips" came about. Slips were small designs worked on canvas, and subsequently cut out and mounted on a ground fabric of velvet. It meant that far less stitching was necessary and the velvet was a far softer textile to drape than canvas covered with stitchery.

In the 18th century, the fashion for mahogany lent itself to the dramatic carving of flowers, fruit, chinoiserie and singerie (monkeys). Painted and gilded furniture, and marble and inlay techniques, made furniture decorative enough without needlework upholstery. Thus pictures, pole screens (small screens to shield one's

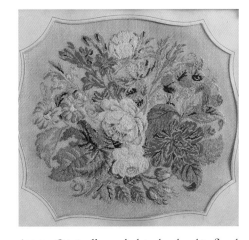

ABOVE Originally worked in beads, this floral design uses a Berlin woolwork chart. Berlin woolwork was particularly popular during the mid-18th century in England and America.

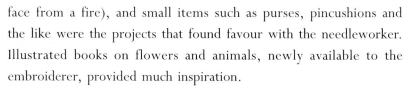

face from a fire), and small items such as purses, pincushions and the like were the projects that found favour with the needleworker. Illustrated books on flowers and animals, newly available to the embroiderer, provided much inspiration.

Many of the items featured in this book are from this period or are inspired by it: the Delft picture is dated 1715, and the dolls' house rug is taken from the original Axminster carpet at Harewood House, Yorkshire, England.

Berlin woolwork became very popular in the 19th century. At that time there was a major change in men's work with many more going out to a factory or office. In the past, most trades and professions were carried out from the home. Many women had more time on their hands, and printed magazines and journals – with embroidery and needlepoint charts for the reader to copy – became widely available for the first time.

Even within the Berlin woolwork craze there were definite trends that help us to date pieces – the introduction of aniline dyes in the 1850s being a fundamental factor. The fashion for building hot-houses and palm courts in public buildings in the latter part of the 19th century made it possible to grow exotic plants. Needleworkers were quick to select designs with orchids and lilies, and forgo the roses and garden flowers that had, until then, been popular – so the type of flower in a design helps us to date it. Stitching either a complete design (see the Country Bouquet on perforated paper – page 58), or just highlights, with beads was yet another fashion for the avid stitcher to follow.

Toward the end of the century, the Arts and Crafts movement was extremely influential in creating better design.

BELOW This cushion is based on a design found in the Mary Dowell Pattern Piece – an immense sampler stitched during the 1800s. Samplers were a testbed for new stitches and motifs and also highlighted the ability of needlewomen.

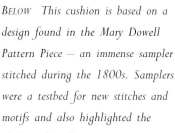

In England, the Royal School of Needlework (originally called the School of Art Needlework) was founded under the presidency of H.R.H. the Princess Christian of Schleswig-Holstein, the daughter of Queen Victoria of Great Britain. (Hence, the majority of the cushion designs found in this book are named after Queen Victoria's children.) This inspired organizations such as the Needlework School of the Museum of Fine Arts in Boston to encourage the art-needlework movement in America.

From the earliest types of needlework, the items stitched and the designs selected have always had a very close relationship with the current needs, fashions and availability of materials. Today is no exception, as people want to relax with something that does not need a great deal of equipment.

If you are relatively new to needlepoint, short one-day instruction courses are often available to help you to improve techniques and to learn new stitches. Throughout America there are chapters of two guilds — the American Needlepoint Guild and the Embroiderers' Guild, both of whom hold regular workshops. Similarly, residential courses are always very popular, be they in the English Lake District or the sunshine of Spain. In France, a visit to the Cluny Museum in Paris would very worthwhile — it houses a wonderful historical collection of textiles and tapestries.

Whether you copy the following projects exactly, adapt them for your own purposes, or simply admire the beautiful photographs, I do hope you enjoy this book.

ABOVE After the restoration of Charles II of England in 1660, the increase in popularity of walnut furniture meant that table carpets soon became floor rugs. The rug shown features an ever-popular tartan pattern.

Before you begin

A completed piece of needlepoint is not achieved overnight, and the selection of the correct materials is crucial to both the pleasure had while stitching and the success of the finished result.

All the projects in this book list the required materials and the order of work. Follow these instructions carefully, otherwise the finished size of the work will differ and the ply of the chosen thread will have to be adjusted.

ESSENTIALS
Canvas
Most good-quality canvas is 100 per cent cotton, but pure linen is also available in fine mesh. The fineness of any canvas is indicated by a number (14, 16, 18, etc). This is the number of threads to the inch; thus 14-mesh has less threads and therefore bigger holes than 18-mesh. Canvases of 24- and even 28-mesh were popular with canvas-workers up until the beginning of the 19th century, but the pieces illustrated in this book all use 14- or 18-mesh canvas. Each project lists the mesh of canvas needed to obtain the same size as the design photographed.

There are two main types of canvas: Penelope or double thread, and mono or single thread. The mono canvas is available both with

an evenweave (sometimes called regular) or interlocked thread. Mono evenweave cotton canvas made by Zweigart has been used for all the projects in the book.

Do not be tempted to use interlock canvas: it looks similar to evenweave but, on close inspection, you can see that at each intersection the threads are bonded together rather than weaving over and under each other as with evenweave. Once interlock canvas is at all out of shape it is almost impossible to get it straight again, even if it is stretched a number of times. Neither is there any "give" to the finished piece; if you sat on a chair or cushion worked on interlock canvas a thread could snap easily, leaving a hole in the seat.

Canvas is generally available in white and antique brown. The colour is a personal choice, although if you wish to work in a dark colour scheme brown is more satisfactory; for a pale scheme, white is the best choice.

Canvas is available in different widths: 68cm (27in) and 1m (40in) are the most common. An especially wide measure – 136cm (54in) – is marvellous for rugs and wall-hangings worked in one piece. (See additional comments under the Rugs section, pages 72–89.)

LEFT There is a wide range of threads currently available on the market, although wool undoubtedly is the most durable.

The canvas should be cut 10cm (4in) wider and deeper than the finished design; that is, with a 5cm (2in) border all around. Finish all the cut edges before starting work: either use a double row of machine-stitching or bind the edges with 2.5cm (1in) masking tape.

THREADS

Wool undoubtedly gives the longest wear. This can be seen from many antique pieces where the wool stitches are still in place while those originally worked in silk are long gone. Wool is therefore recommended for all upholstery pieces or rugs. Decorative pieces such as pictures or fire screens that will not receive much wear can look wonderful in cottons or silks.

Each project in this book is matched to the original as closely as possible with wool that is available today and, where appropriate, other threads have been suggested.

To avoid confusion with the different thicknesses in which the various threads are available, the word ply is used when giving the unit or correct amount of yarn (whether wool, cotton or silk) for each stitch. Ply is taken to mean the thinnest strand of the yarn you can take apart easily.

The majority of projects in this book (except for some of the antique pieces that we have charted) list the quantities of thread needed if you are working the design on the mesh specified. However, if you decide to change the mesh size you will need to re-calculate the amount of wool or other threads needed. Everyone's tension and stitching habits vary, so the way to make sure that calculations are accurate is

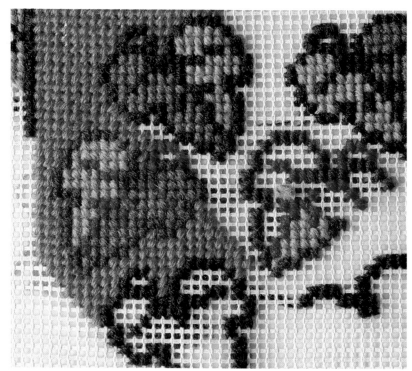

to stitch a square 2.5 x 2.5cm (1 x 1in) in the actual stitch you plan to use and to work out from that how much thread you will need for the whole design. As a very rough rule of thumb, a 25g (1oz) hank of wool enables you to make about 15 x 15cm (6 x 6in) with basketweave tent stitch (see page 20) on 14-mesh canvas; the same amount of wool will cover about 13 x 13cm (5 x 5in) when you are working Florentine stitches (because of the extra ply needed for good coverage).

It is worthwhile getting more than enough of a background colour as any dye-lot change will show far more than a slight difference within a pattern.

Wool

Two different brands of wool have been used for the projects in the book: Appleton's Crewel and DMC Medici; both of them come in single

ABOVE 7-mesh canvas.
RIGHT Fine canvas is good for samplers, where much of the canvas is left exposed.

ply and are combined in a number of ply at the same time in the needle to provide good coverage. Another brand, Paterna Persian, also comes in strands of 3 ply that are easy to separate and use in the correct quantities but, while being of excellent quality, it tends to have a more modern colour range.

Appleton's Crewel has both colour-range names and numbers while Medici has shade numbers only; both are standard worldwide. The correct number of plies for each stitch is given for each project. If you substitute one brand of wool for another or move to a finer or coarser canvas, experiment until you find the number of plies that gives good coverage of the canvas with your particular tension. When working with a very dark colour, an extra ply might also be necessary to cover the canvas completely. Appleton's Crewel is an English wool that has an excellent range of shades in each colour family, making it ideal for detailed shading and Florentine work. It is available in two quantities: a 25g (1oz) hank and a very small skein which is useful if only a few stitches of a shade are needed. When working on 18-mesh or coarser canvas, cut new hanks into two equal lengths to get a good working amount. When working on a finer canvas, cut the wool into three equal lengths: there will be more friction on the wool as it passes through the holes of the fine canvas and a long length would wear thin before it was finished.

DMC Medici is a French wool, originally made for the manufacture of Aubusson carpets and woven tapestries. It has a smaller colour range than Appleton's Crewel but the natural earth and traditional shades associated with antique pieces are particularly good.

The colour names given in the projects here are purely descriptive and added to help you; shops will go by the manufacturer's reference number. Medici is available in 50g (2oz) hanks (that are further divisible into five hanks) and small skeins which are useful for the odd stitch or if you wish to experiment with a colour scheme before paying out money for any big project.

Stranded cotton
The DMC range has been used throughout the projects that require stranded cotton. They are all 6-ply divisible and come in 8m (9yd) skeins.

When using stranded cotton, note that there is an "up" and a "down" to the thread. Look at the two paper wrappers; on one there are a pair of hands with one of them pulling the thread to the right. That is the end from which to pull the thread; it might need a little shake to fall free. Cut a length of about 50cm (20in), and always thread the end you have just cut through the eye of the needle as it will tend to reduce kinking in the thread.

Whether you cut the complete skein into working lengths before you begin to stitch is up to you. However, some stitches in the book require a number of ply other than the six in the strand: the Florentine Tulip on page 44, for example, needs 9-ply. The most economic method is to cut three lengths at once and divide one between the other two. If 4-ply is needed, cut two lengths and you will have enough to fill three needles.

Stranded cotton also needs to be "stripped" before use. Cut the length(s) and assemble the correct number of plies, tie a knot at the bottom; place the knot between the index and middle finger of your left hand with the thread falling forward toward your thumb. With the tip of a needle in your right hand, use it to pick out and separate the individual plies letting them fall over the back of your left hand. When they are all pulled apart (the knot will have kept them together at the end), thread your needle. Stripping

makes the thread lie smoothly on the canvas and gives better coverage. If you need proof of the benefits of this chore, strip one strand of 6-ply and compare it over your finger with a length straight off the skein.

Pearl cotton

The reference numbers in this book refer to the DMC range. It is a softly twisted, single-ply thread in various thicknesses. No. 3 is fairly thick and is good on 12-mesh canvas; No. 5 (used in this book) is good on 14-, 16- and 18-mesh. No.5 is available in 25m (27½yd) skeins and 48m (52½yd) balls. Use the thread as is. To prepare a new skein for use, take off the two paper wrappers, untwist the skein and cut through it twice, at the knot holding it together and at the opposite end, giving two equal lengths.

NEEDLES

Use a blunt-tipped tapestry needle.

NEEDLE SIZE	CANVAS MESH
18	7 and 10
20	14
22	16 and 18
24	22 and 24

Generally, these needles are available either in mixed-size packets or all in one size. Single sizes are often the most convenient to buy, as on the canvases specified here you only need size 20 and 22 needles.

SCISSORS

Two pairs are essential: embroidery scissors with sharp points and a

RIGHT Some of the equipment that adds enjoyment to stitching, including frame, scissors and buttons.

larger pair for cutting hanks of wool and canvas.

FRAMES

Essential for canvas work, frames make work easier to see, keep the stitch tension smoother and help reduce distortion of the canvas. There are various types, but the simplest and most adaptable is assembled from artist's stretcher bars, available from art supply stores. These are bought in pairs of varying lengths which simply slot together. They can be used time and time again and reassembled in other combinations. When working a large project, such as a rug, it is best to use a frame no larger than a 45cm (18in)-square, and simply move it around carefully. Mount the canvas as taut as possible and, if you

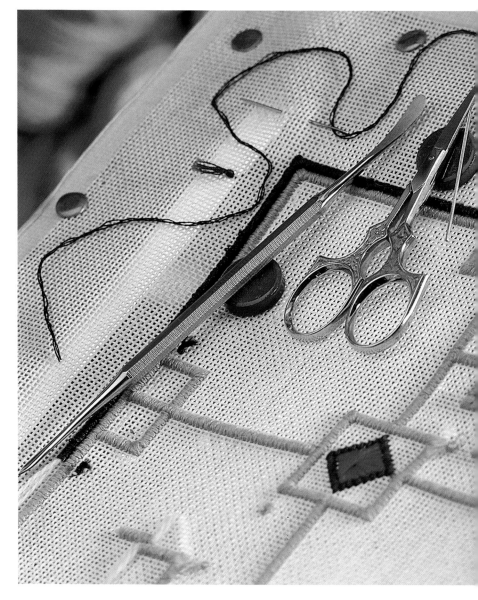

use artists' stretcher bars, use flat-headed drawing pins (thumb tacks) rather than staples for fixing; this enables the canvas to be re-stretched if it gets loose at any time.

ADDITIONAL EQUIPMENT

Extras can be quite expensive so, frequently, what not to buy becomes an important decision. However, if you get better results

by using a particular tool or are more comfortable stitching with a good stand or lamp, try to buy it. Remember that the single most expensive thing you invest in your needlework is your time — so you should enjoy doing it.

There are certain items that are particularly handy:

Metal needle threader: with two different size hooks for wool and finer threads. (A wire one for sewing cotton collapses at the first go.)

Set of magnetic buttons: there are various shapes on the market but those which come in a pack of four are really strong and leave no marks on your delicate work. Simply place a pair, one above and one below the canvas and use them to "park" tools such as needles, scissors, threader etc.

Laying tool: something that can smooth the threads just before it goes down onto the canvas — makes all the difference to Florentine stitchery with stranded or pearl cotton.

Good light: essential for stitching. A small lamp that can be angled onto the work is vital. However, there are some lamps with built-in magnification that are wonderful. There are three main types: those with a heavy floor or table base, those that clamp onto a table or desk and the newest — that fit onto a stainless-steel floor base. Choice is personal and depends on space and funds available.

Floor frames: also come in different sizes and forms. Before buying, research your options and try some out if possible. My favourite is the stainless-steel variety. What is particularly useful — a point to

consider when selecting any floor frame — is that the height adjusts easily to allow you to sit in any chair. Also, the base is to one side so, when you need to get up you simply push the work to one side and stand up, and it is easy to turn to the back of the work to finish off threads. Finally, if you wish to switch from project to project you can do so extremely quickly with this particular stand.

PREPARING TO WORK

For some designs you may be more comfortable marking out certain guide marks onto the canvas before starting work. Projects where this is suggested are Frederick's Florentine (page 30), Sewing Bag (page 114) and Tartan Rug (page 78). For these straight-line guides, use an HB or harder pencil: the sharp point will run smoothly along a channel between two canvas threads.

When marking a curvilinear design, such as the Floral Runner on page 100, use a permanent waterfast pen with a fine tip.

It is always worth test-marking a small area of the actual canvas you plan to use. Size, a stiffener that is used in the finishing of the canvas, can float off and take any ink marks into the stitchery. Therefore, test-mark the canvas, allow the ink to dry, wet the canvas and blot the area with white kitchen paper. If any mark comes off onto the paper, do not use that pen on that canvas.

Never mark a canvas on which you are going to work one of the lacy backgrounds or will be leaving the background bare. For example, with the Victorian stitch sampler (see page 62), use a tacking thread to mark the central point down the length of the piece, and only mark any guides on the extreme edge of the canvas, which will be cut off in the making-up process.

FOLLOWING THE CHARTS

The great advantage with the charts in this book is that while the mesh size has been specified, it allows you to select another mesh if you prefer. In order to purchase the correct amount of canvas of a different mesh, count the stitches on the relevant chart (horizontal and vertical), then divide these figures by the count of the chosen canvas. For example, if a chart counts 180 x 360 stitches and you want to work on 18-mesh canvas, the design will be 26 x 51cm (10 x 20in). Then add on the required background area, plus 10cm (4in) on both sides, to calculate the size of cut canvas.

The colours specified have been closely matched to the originals, but all old pieces of needlework fade and some colours change in bright sunlight or even just constant use. You may prefer to substitute alternative colours.

Quantities of thread have been listed, where possible. For other projects, the quantities needed will depend on the canvas chosen, how much of the design you decide to work and how much background you allow. Everyone's tension is different and some people are far more extravagant than others. The sure way to find out how much you will need is to test-stitch a square 2.5cm (1in) on the chosen canvas, and then calculate the areas of each colour.

The colour keys that accompany the charts give the colour and the thread reference number. ACW= Appletons Crewel wool, DMC = stranded or pearl cotton and MWA = Medici Wool Art.

STARTING AND FINISHING A THREAD

To start a thread, knot the end and stitch in from the right side of the work, placing the knot about 4cm (1½in) away and facing the direction in which you will be working toward. When the stitching reaches the knot, it can be snipped off as the tail under the work will have been caught by the back of the stitches. To finish a thread, weave the thread through the back of a number of stitches.

For lacy stitches the procedure is different, as no row should be started without enough thread to finish it; starting and finishing should be done in surrounding solid stitches. Basketweave tent stitch is also different: see special instructions on page 20.

CORDS AND TASSELS

Cords, plaits and tassels made from matching wool or cotton add a tremendous decorator touch to many projects – including cushions and bell pulls or runners.

Cords

These are best made on a small machine, but can be made by hand – although two pairs of hands really help.

Cut two pieces of yarn, in different colours, approximately five times the final length needed. Knot the ends together and trim the knot neatly. Place the knot in a central position and place a pencil in each loop, at either end. Holding the yarn taut at all times, twist it by rotating the pencils in opposite directions, both at the same speed. When the cord is twisted quite tight, still holding it taut, one person should take the knot in the centre and

give the other person their end with the pencil. Gradually release the cord at the non-pencil end and twisting the first few centimetres (inches) counter-clockwise, then hand over hand, release it 5cm (2in) at a time, smoothing down the length. It will twist itself into a cord ready to be used.

If you need to repeat a cord – for a pair of cushions, for example – keep a note of what you used and the number of twists made.

Plaits

These can be made single-handedly, and the eight-strand version is most attractive for upholstery as well as cushions.

On average, you will need to cut lengths about three times longer than the finished length. One, two or four colours can be used, but each should be of the same thickness.

Gather the lengths of all the yarn together, align the ends and fold in half. Tie them together at the fold with strong thread and secure them to something firm with a large safety pin. Group the strands of the same colour together, fanning them out from the safety pin, balancing the colours on either side.

Now plait the colours, taking first one outside group of threads to the centre, and then the other outside group, in the same way, creating a thick flat plait.

Tassels

Any combination of colours and thread, wool, pearl or stranded cotton, metallic thread or even narrow ribbons can be used; however, each thread should be uncut. A simple tassel is described here but having made a few you will quickly discover ways to make them even more eye-catching with beads embroidery, lace and so on.

Cut a piece of firm card about 10cm (4in) wide, and 2.5 times the length of the finished tassel. Fold it with the two 10cm (4in) sides together. Wind the threads around the card, starting at the open side. If you plan a multi-coloured tassel it is important to wind all the colours together as this will avoid a clump of individual colours in the finished tassel. If you are making a number of matching tassels, count the winds so that they all match.

When the required thickness is achieved, thread a needle with a 10cm (4in) length of strong thread in a matching colour and tie all the threads together on the fold of the cardboard. Cut the other ends of the threads (this is made easier by the card being open).

Wrap another length – about 25cm (10in) – of matching or contrasting thread about one-third of the way down the tassel, to form the neck. If you want a decorative neck, this wrapping can be button-holed right around, a string of beads added or a short length of ribbon or lace and stitched in place with a sharp needle. Trim the base of the tassel evenly and use a large-toothed comb to fluff the threads out.

MAKING UP CUSHIONS

Cushions are a beautiful way of showing off needlepoint, and are relatively easy to make. Use fabric such as velvet, with the stitched piece mounted in the centre of one side and leave a fabric border, about 2.5cm/1in wide all around.

1 Buy a cushion pad of the appropriate size for your piece of needlepoint: 2.5cm/1in larger on each side. Cut two pieces of fabric the same size as the pad, plus 1.5cm/⅝in on all four sides for seams.

2 Carefully hand-stitch the finished needlepoint in the centre of one of the pieces of fabric, trimming and turning under the raw edges, as necessary.

3 For the opening in the cushion cover, fold over to the wrong side, on one side of each piece of fabric, 1.5cm/⅝in.

4 Put the two pieces right sides and folded edges together, and pin around three sides, 1.5cm/⅝in in from the raw edges. Then machine-stitch.

5 Turn the cover over to the right side, insert the cushion pad, and then carefully hand-sew the opening closed. Hand-sew cord around all four sides, if desired.

MAKING UP TIE-BACKS

Making up a tie-back is not complicatied. There are three basic shapes for stiffened tie-backs: straight (like that of the tie-back on page 106), gentle curved and gentle curved with a scalloped lower edge. For most designs, the gentle curve looks best with needlepoint. However, if individual posies or flowers were placed within each curve of a scalloped tie-back it could look spectacular.

The stiffening is usually buckram, cut to the same shape as the worked canvas. When the design is complete and stretched in the usual

way, turn the unworked edges of the canvas over the buckram (they may need trimming or notching, depending upon the shape) and attach a fabric backing. A piped edge in a co-ordinating plain can look smart, or a hand-made cord from the same wool as the stitching would finish them off beautifully. Attach a ring at either end; the one on the leading edge should be inset so it will not be seen in place.

The hooks on the window frame to take the tie-backs must be positioned carefully, in order to get the proportions of the curtains right and not loose too much light. As a general rule, the base of the tie-back should be positioned two-thirds of the way down the curtain.

Tie-backs are not restricted to window curtains. Dress curtains either side of a bed could be trimmed with tie-backs and, for a truly spectacular effect, show about a corona or crown worked in needlepoint, with the curtains sweeping out from it and held back with a pair of tie-backs in a co-ordinating pattern.

A corona would not be difficult to make or fix. A typical one, to be fitted high on the wall at the head of the bed, has two parts – a flat disc which should be oval (about 38 x 23cm/ 15 x 9in) with a straight back to go against the wall and the pelmet, in this case the worked canvas mounted on buckram. The disc can be fixed with brackets to the wall (which must be strong enough to take the weight of the curtains and canvas) and should have a curved track to take the curtains.

BASIC STITCHES AND PATTERNS

The following pages concentrate upon the many different stitches used in needlepoint. Although tent stitch is the most common, many other needlepoint stitches can be worked.

Tent/Basketweave

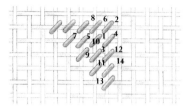

This stitch can be worked in any area, however small, because it is very hard-wearing and acts with the threads of the canvas for additional strength. It is always worked on the diagonal, hence its other name: diagonal tent stitch. On evenweave or regular canvas (which is recommended for almost all projects in this book) there is an added tip to help you get perfectly smooth basketweave stitching. Look closely at the canvas and you will see that the threads pass over and under each other at each intersection. By using these intersections to guide your stitching, you will always know whether you should be going up or down. They help you to find your way across a motif such as a flower or monogram, and you will never make the mistake of working two rows up or down, side by side. Starting and finishing a thread for all other stitches is explained on page 18. However, a special method is needed for basketweave; if an up row is being worked, take the old thread horizontally out to the unworked area of canvas on the left and bring the

new thread in vertically from above (catching just the backs of stitches on the reverse). If a down row is being worked, then you should bring the old thread down vertically (into the unworked area of canvas) and the new thread in from the right through to the back of the stitches in a horizontal row.

Continental tent

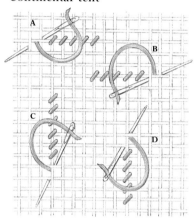
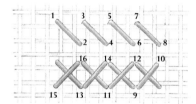

Similar to basketweave tent stitch, but is worked only when a single line (vertical, horizontal or diagonal) is required. The diagram above shows continental tent stitch worked in a horizontal row in both directions, and vertically both up and down; it always has a long stitch behind the work. If a diagonal line is needed, you will find that on the lower left to upper right slant, each of the stitches touch; on the other slant, upper left to lower right, they do not. It is possible to make this particular angle optically correct by running a long stitch in the same thread under all the worked stitches on the right side of the canvas to "join" them up. Stitches at this angle occur in some letters, ie. the second stroke of a capital A.

Florentine patterns

These use a zig-zag pattern, often in graduated colours, and have always been popular with needleworkers, and so a number of projects in this book use them. Traditionally, they are made up of upright stitches and the individual pattern is varied by the length of the stitch and the number of stitches in each group. Whatever the canvas mesh, it is necessary to use an extra ply of wool or other thread: that is, above the number that will give sufficient coverage with tent stitch. When combining it with other stitches, such as straight gobelin, the stitches will share canvas holes.

Cross stitch

This can be worked quite satisfactorily in two different ways. The first method is to work a row of half-crosses, all slanting on the same angle right across the area and then return completing the second and top stitch on the bisecting diagonal. The diagram above shows this. There will be a short stitch behind the first stage and a long one behind the second; this makes for a hard-wearing piece of canvaswork. The alternative method is to complete each cross in turn before moving on to the next one. However, the first method (as shown) is preferable, as it is much easier to make sure that all the crosses have the top stitch at the same angle.

Long-legged cross (Binding)

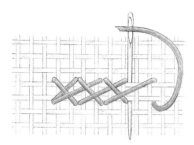

The diagram shows how to work a straight row. Start each row from the left with cross stitch; thread goes vertically under the canvas. Finish the row with another cross. When binding the canvas, remove it from the frame, fold and stitch a long-legged cross through both layers.

Crossed corner stitch

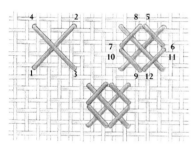

Work base cross over four canvas threads, working the top (second) stitch on the same diagonal. Work four tipping stitches in order given in either the same or contrasting thread according to the project.

Skip tent

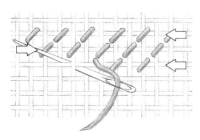

Work these after other areas are complete. Carefully follow diagram; there is very little thread behind the work and the second and subsequent rows form a diagonal line on canvas.

Straight gobelin

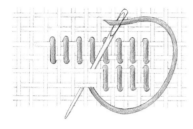

An upright stitch that can be worked over several threads. If it is worked as a border, work five stitches at each corner down into the same hole making the exact corner stitch (at 45°) last. This pattern can look very attractive.

Sloping gobelin 1

Sloping gobelin 2

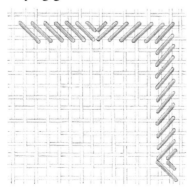

Sloping gobelin is a stitch that, like the straight variation, can be worked over any number of threads. The angle of the stitches is frequently reversed at the central point on each side of a border. We have shown the different angles in the illustrations.

Victorian pattern darning 1

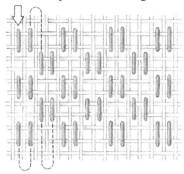

Victorian pattern darning 2

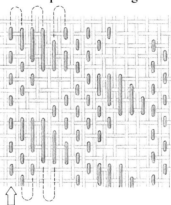

1: Work in vertical rows. Row 1 is worked over two threads under two threads; row 2 (opposite direction) is next to the first. Rows 3 and 4 have stitches to fit beside the spaces created by the first two. Five and six are a repeat of one and two.
2: Requires careful counting. Work the vertical rows at one or other edge so that you are familiar with the count before having to compensate around the shell.

Chain stitch

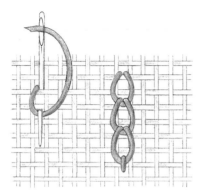

Bring the needle and thread up as shown then go down again in the same hole leaving a loop on the surface of the canvas. Come up two threads away inside the loop. Repeat, going down in this hole again. When end of row is reached, take last stitch outside last loop.

Tartan

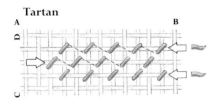

Before starting, mark the top two corners of canvas 'A' and 'B'; quarter-turn the canvas and mark the top corners 'C' and 'D' – with 'D' in the same corner as 'A'. With the canvas held with AB at the top, follow the chart. Work back and forth across the canvas with very little thread behind the work; the stitches form a diagonal line on the canvas as shown. Only when the area is complete, quarter-turn to the CD position and repeat exactly, working a stitch at the same angle where there are none. By always working from the right-hand end, you will come up in empty holes.

Diagonal tartan

Above: stitches in both AB and CD position. Mark canvas as with tartan; in AB position work basketweave tent diagonally up and down the canvas. Work alternate rows; these stitches will slant to the right. When the area is complete turn to CD position and repeat colours.

Waffle stitch

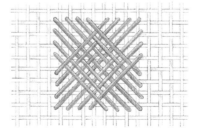

Work waffle stitch as shown in the diagram above. Following the numbers, work the large diagonal cross over eight threads 1-2 and 3-4. Continue to work the diagonal stitches parallel to 1-2

and 3-4 continuing to follow the numbers. Pass stitch 27-28 under 21-22 before completing the stitch.

Waffle and Hungarian stitch

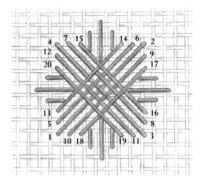

Used in Victorian Stitch Sampler. Work the large diagonal cross over eight threads following the numbers on the chart. Pass 19-20 under 13-14 before completing this stitch. When this is complete, work the four groups of Hungarian stitch in the contrast colour.

Rhodes stitch

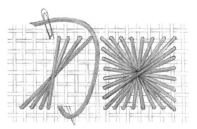

Above left shows the stitch worked over 7 canvas threads and subsequent stitches worked into each hole with a long stitch behind the work as shown by the needle. On the right you can see the complete stitch worked. Rhodes stitch can be worked over any number of threads, 8, 10 and 12, for example.

Couching 1

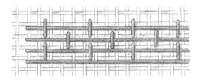

Couching 2

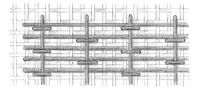

Couching 3

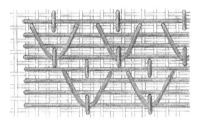

Couching is a technique which involves a thick or metallic thread being sewn onto the ground fabric using a different, and generally finer, thread. The three couching patterns used in the Victorian stitch sampler (see page 62) are all examples of surface couching.

Ribbed spiders

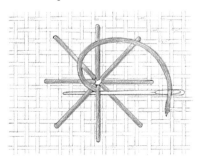

Set up the spokes going down into the centre. Bring up the needle between two spokes and weave on the surface back over one spoke, forward under two. Continue until all the spokes are tightly packed.

Mosaic stitch

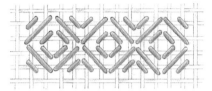

Mosaic stitch consists of groups of three diagonal stitches, over 1, 2 and 1 canvas threads are worked at alternate angles as shown in the diagram above. Four groups of three form a larger square, as shown.

Hungarian stitch

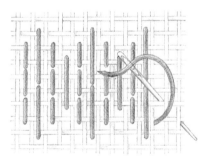

Work from left to right. Bring thread through to the right side of canvas and stitch up over two threads. Move 1 thread to the right and 1 thread down, making a vertical stitch over 4 threads. Move 1 thread to right and 1 thread higher than the previous stitch, and then another vertical over two threads. Move two threads to right; repeat to end of row. Next row, interlocked, is worked in a contrasting colour.

Diagonal Florence

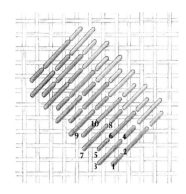

Work diagonally, lower right to upper left. Stitches are over 1, 2 and 1 canvas threads. On the second and subsequent rows, a short stitch shares with a stitch over 2 from the previous row.

Russian stitch

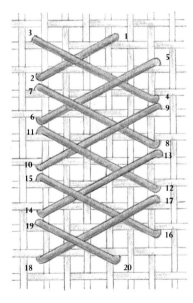

Russian stitch should be worked from the top area down – following the numbers shown on the diagram above. Behind the work, there is only a short stitch. (Russian stitch can be found in the Victorian stitch sampler on page 62.)

Cushions

Parterre cushion

Very little is known about this design. Its strong colours indicate the use of aniline dyes, dating it to about 1860. It was originally worked in wools and the background in beads – which was unusual as beads were normally used for the main subject of the pattern (often flowers) or all worked in beads.

The original is thought to be a kit or a printed chart. It is reminiscent of two design sources: stained glass windows and gardens (formal knot gardens or a parterre).

Geometrical flower and vegetable beds that were outlined with neat box hedges were popular in France during the 16th century, and these quickly found favour in Elizabethan houses. Ladies were not slow to translate these intricate patterns into needlework. The flowers stitched within the circles also help to date the piece. Early in the century the designs usually included roses, pansies and auriculas – flowers the embroiderer would know from her own garden. However, with the development of the green- or palm-house, flowers that appeared all winter quickly replaced the more commonplace blooms.

LEFT AND ABOVE Embroiderers have always been influenced by trends in horticulture, as can be seen from this vivid cushion. The iridescent background beautifully sets off the bright shades of the flowers.

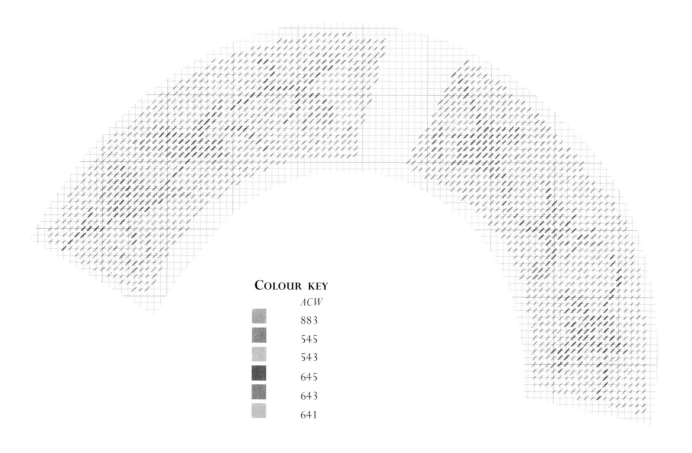

COLOUR KEY

ACW

883
545
543
645
643
641

ABILITY LEVEL Intermediate

FINISHED SIZE
38 x 38cm/15 x 15in

THREAD
Appleton's crewel wool

NEEDLE SIZE 22

CANVAS 18-mesh

STITCHES Tent

WORKING THE DESIGN
Follow the chart (we have isolated
the main motif) and colour key.

An interesting challenge would be to
recreate this whole design using

flowers from other projects in the
book. First enlarge the "road map"
on page 28 to 38 x 38cm/15 x 15in
square and trace the circles onto the
18-mesh canvas. The finished work
will look best if you line up the
outside edge of all three curves
along each side of the design. Other
than that, accurate thread counting is
not necessary. Only the shades of
wool for the ivy leaves are given and
you will obviously choose suitable
colours for the flowers worked in
the curved areas. If you wish to
work the circles and curves in
Appleton's Crewel to match the
original, the gold is Honeysuckle 3
(693), the blues are Sky 5 and 7
(565 & 567), the red "seaweed"
shape is Scarlet 1 & 3 (501 & 503).

The background could be worked in
DMC Ecru Pearl Cotton no.5, or
crewel wool Pastel 883 rather than
the small beads as the original.

Copy the chart for the ivy leaves
in the areas that correspond to the
chart above. Turn this chart upside
down to work the other two areas.

To choose motifs to work in the
various areas, count the threads
available and select designs that will
fit. You do not necessarily have to
work a complete group as one or
two flowers from another design
could be just what is needed.
Similarly, an initial or monogram
could be planned for the middle,
and something simple (like Diagonal
Florence, page 23) could be worked
in the four corner areas.

Frederick's florentine

This design is mid-Victorian. Like the following two cushion designs, it is based on parts of a huge sampler, known as the Mary Dowell Pattern Piece. Mary Dowell was the wife of a vicar who lived in a small Norfolk village from 1848–96. During this time, all her guests were encouraged to stitch a small pattern or motif which she then pieced together. There are over 1,000 patterns on 400 different canvas patches stitched into a "visitors' book" sampler that measures 12.5m (41ft) long. It starts at one end with fine canvas and naturally dyed wools stitched in small delicate designs including flowers, Florentine patterns, repeating patterns and intricate pastoral scenes. Later, with the introduction of coarser canvas, cross stitch and aniline dyes, the designs become larger, bolder and the colours brighter.

The pattern used here is variously called Florentine, Bargello or Hungarian Point. This sort of patterning is found chiefly in Hungary, North Italy, England and America. Being comparatively fast-growing, it has always been the first choice for large upholstery, rugs and even wall-panelling for complete rooms. The stitching never wears as well as the tight tent stitch, but if care is taken in selecting a pattern with stitches not too long, rugs and upholstery will give good service and be much faster to complete. In fact, this design, repeated a number of times, would make an attractive rug.

Traditional Florentine/Bargello has stitches of all one length while Hungarian Point has the same straight stitches but of varying lengths within the same row. The design here has a Florentine border and a Hungarian Point centre.

RIGHT This cushion uses the original colours found on the Mary Dowell sampler. If you wish to try your own scheme, select the wools carefully as the colours in the background to the border must be very strong to look effective.

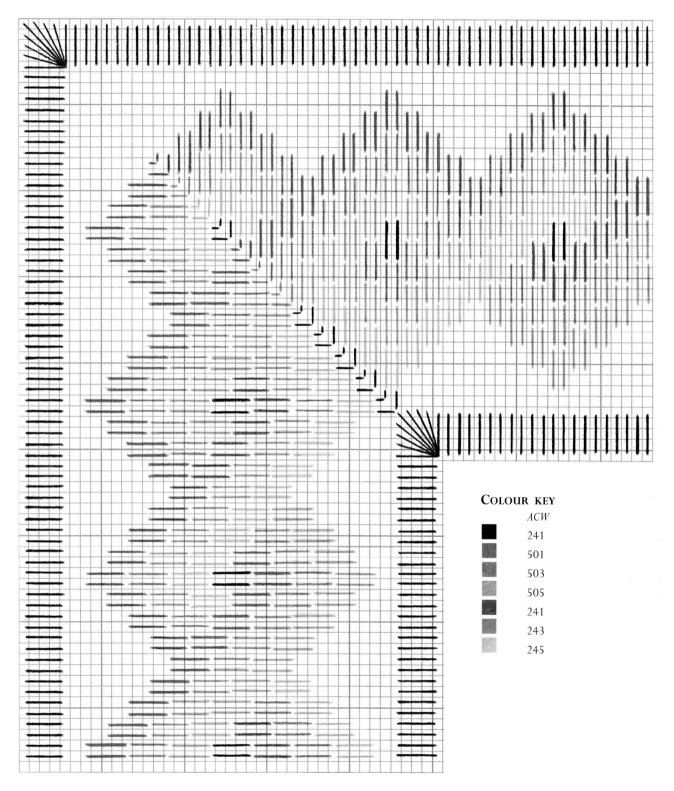

COLOUR KEY

ACW

241
501
503
505
241
243
245

ABILITY LEVEL
Intermediate

FINISHED SIZE
33 x 36cm/13 x 14in

THREAD/QUANTITIES
Appleton's Crewel Wool

Colour	No	Hanks
Black	241	1½
Olive	241	½
	243	½
	245	½
Scarlet	501	½
	503	½
	505	½
Heraldic	841	¼ (or 2 skeins)
	842	¼ (or 2 skeins)
	844	¼ (or 2 skeins)
Wine	711	¼ (or 2 skeins)
	713	¼ (or 2 skeins)
Off-white	992	1

NEEDLE SIZE 20

CANVAS 14-mesh

STITCHES
Florentine, straight gobelin

NOTE: Background (filler) stitches are not shown on the chart provided on page 32.

WORKING THE DESIGN
1 Use 4-ply crewel wool throughout.

2 Find the middle of the canvas by folding, and mark it with a small pencil cross. Count up and down from the centre: 51 threads, then 4, then 32, then another 4. Then count out to both sides: 60, 4, 32, 4. Mark the centre of each side on the edge of the canvas.

3 Following the "road map" below, set up the lozenge outlines in the central area with black. Start in the middle (where your small cross is) with a stitch over 6 canvas threads.

4 Again using black, work the inner straight gobelin border over 4 canvas threads as shown on the chart on page 32.

5 Now all the infills for the lozenges can be worked. Refer to the "road map" of the central area. All stitches in areas marked A1 and A2 are identical, but the colour schemes are different. All areas marked B1 and B2 have an identical stitch pattern – but again, colour schemes vary. It is easier to fill in full shapes of each scheme before attempting the half shapes around the edges.

"A" shapes, working inward from outlines already worked:

A1	A2
245	844
243	842
241	841
992	992
503	711

The two stitches in the middle are black.

"B" shapes, working inward from outlines already worked:

B1	B2
505	713
503	711
501	992
992	842
243	844

BORDER
6 The inner row of straight gobelin stitches (shown on the chart on the previous page) has already been worked (see step 4). Now work a mitre line in pencil on the canvas diagonally out from each straight

gobelin corner for 36 canvas threads; this will indicate where to finish the compensations stitches on the main ribbon border, and continue out to the final pencil mark you have already made.

7 Work a row of straight gobelin over 4 canvas threads in the channel that is marked as an outer edge to the design.

8 Next work the ribbon border between these two rows of straight gobelin. Start with the top left-hand corner (with the chart to help you). All the stitches, except for the compensations stitches into the mitre line, are over four canvas threads. [NB. There will be a group of three stitches rather than the usual two, centrally along the top and bottom borders; there will be a single stitch in the middle of both the sides.]

9 When the ribbons are complete, infill with black between the ribbons and straight gobelin stitch (left void on the chart on page 32) and also in the middle of each ribbon turn (shown on the chart); all these stitches are in pairs and are over 4 canvas threads.

ALTERNATIVE COLOUR SCHEMES

Although the colours given here are taken from the original scheme on the Mary Dowell Pattern Piece, it is also very attractive worked in other colourways. Here are just a few for you to try. The colours are given in the same order as those in the thread list on page 33. For example, the mid-blue, dull marine or peacock would be used where it is instructed to use black.

[All alternative schemes use Appleton's Crewel Wool]

SCHEME A

Colour	No	Hanks
Mid-blue	156	1½
Pastel green	873	½
Grey-green	351	½
Jacobean	293	½
Chocolate	181	½
Chocolate	183	½
Chocolate	185	½
Biscuit	761	¼
Putty	982	¼
Elephant	974	¼
Custard	851	¼
Biscuit	764	¼
Mid-blue	152	1

SCHEME B

Colour	No	Hanks
Dull marine	326	1½
Olive	241	½
Olive	243	½
Olive	245	½
Flame	204	½
Flame	206	½
Flame	208	½
Biscuit	761	¼
Biscuit	764	¼
Biscuit	765	¼
Honeysuckle	691	¼
Honeysuckle	693	¼
Off-white	992	1

SCHEME C

Colour	No	Hanks
Sea	406	1½
Flame	204	½
Flame	206	½
Flame	208	½
Honey	692	½
Honey	693	½

Colour	No	Hanks
Heraldic	843	½
Dull marine	322	½
Dull marine	324	¼
Dull marine	325	¼
Putty	982	¼
Elephant	974	¼
Honey	691	1

SCHEME D

Colour	No	Hanks
Flame	204	1½
Flame	206	½
Flame	208	½
Honey	691	½
Honey	693	½
Custard	851	½
Biscuit	761	½
Biscuit	764	¼
Biscuit	765	¼
Peacock	641	¼
Peacock	642	¼
Peacock	644	¼
Chocolate	181	1

COLOUR KEY

	ACW
	241
	992
	501
	503
	505
	841
	842
	844
	241
	243
	245
	711
	713

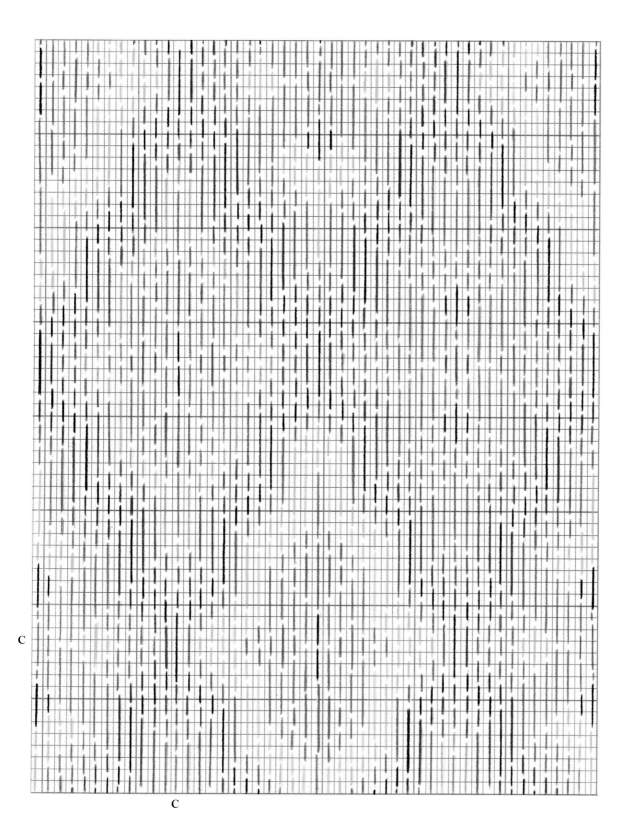

C

C

Leopold's leopard

This particularly striking design – based on a section of the original Mary Dowell Pattern Piece (see page 30) – is taken from two patterns that seem meant for each other. Like the canvas lace work on Vicky's Ribbons (see page 40), this also illustrates the Victorian craze for imitating something in a completely different medium. The fake furs and mock croc of today are nothing new!

The project has been worked, and is shown here, in the original colours. To stitch it, first follow the skeleton chart to set up the pearl-cotton wave/scallop patterns across the central area (see page 38) then fill in the leopard "spots". Next, work the diagonal outlines of the border – turn to the second chart (on page 39) to fill in all these areas. Notice that the columns of red and blue shades alternate between horizontal lines.

On page 24 the same design has been stitched using only shades of one colour – mid-blues – rather than the combination of reds and blue. It is a vivid illustration of just how much colour schemes can play a part in changing the overall look of a piece, possibly making it a more suitable pattern for a home of today.

As with the Frederick's Florentine cushion on page 30, you could work this design using an alternative colour scheme for an equally attractive result. For an appealing alternative, use the following Appleton Crewel Wool threads: Biscuit (761, 1 hank), Biscuit (764, 1 hank), Biscuit (765, 1 hank), Mid-blue (152, ½ hank), Mid-blue (156, ½ hank), Peacock (643, ½ hank), Chocolate (187, 1 hank), Peacock (643, ½ hank).

LEFT This striking design is mid-Victorian and, like the two other cushions in this section of the book, is based on a small section of the immense Mary Dowell Pattern Piece.

ABILITY LEVEL Intermediate

FINISHED SIZE

33 x 33 cm/13 x 13in
["C" denotes centre of chart]

THREAD/QUANTITIES

APPLETON'S CREWEL WOOL

Colour	No	Hanks
Biscuit	761	1
Biscuit	764	1
Biscuit	765	1
Sky-blue	561	½
Sky-blue	563	½
Sky-blue	564	½
Black	993	1
Scarlet	503	½
Flame red	208	½
Bright terracotta	224	½
DMC PEARL COTTON NO. 5		
Ecru	–	2

NEEDLE SIZE 20

CANVAS 14-mesh in brown

STITCHES

Diagonal and continental tent

WORKING THE DESIGN

1 Use 3-ply wool and 2 strands of pearl cotton throughout. Find the middle of the canvas by folding, and mark it with a small pencil cross.

2 Refer to chart 1 which shows the lower left corner of the design. The middle point of the design, which will match with the pencil cross on the canvas, is shown with a large upright cross. Count down from the middle point 12 threads and make the first stitch in the pearl cotton over this canvas thread then follow the chart to the left. Return to the middle and work a mirror image to the right. Continue to work all waves in pearl cotton.

3 Now work all the stitches in black: the leopard spots in both the waves, both sides of the border, and the diagonal bars of the border. Notice how the spot on the inside edge of the border matches the spot on the outside edge of the border and that the spots reverse themselves after the central point.

4 Refer to chart 2 (opposite) which shows large details of the left corner of the design. Note how the stripe colours go the odd stitch into the leopard wave and also how the position of the red and blue bands with black in-between alternates from row to row.

C

C

COLOUR KEY

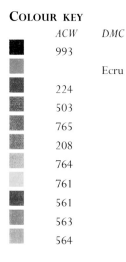

	ACW	DMC
	993	
		Ecru
	224	
	503	
	765	
	208	
	764	
	761	
	561	
	563	
	564	

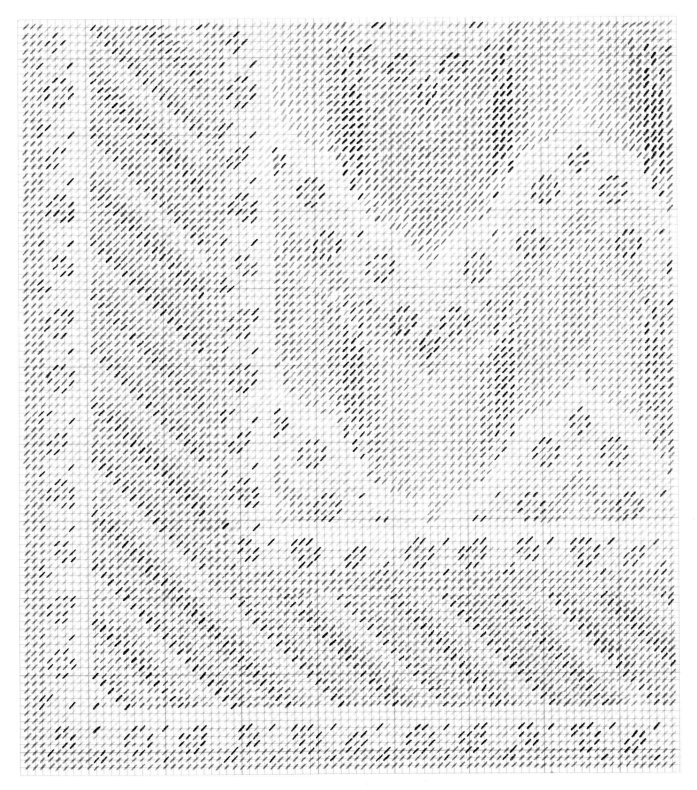

Vicky's ribbons

This pattern of interweaving ribbons was originally worked in primary shades of red, green, blue and yellow with the border in black. The lace-like patterns in the surround were very popular around 1850 and were usually worked in black silk with the rest of the design in wool. This typified the Victorian craze for making one fabric imitate another.

The original design forms part of the Mary Dowell Pattern Piece (see page 30) and was worked entirely in cross stitch. In my adaptation long-legged cross, mosaic and skip tent stitches have been introduced to make the work more interesting and enjoyable to stitch. You may decide to deviate from the original and leave the background bare behind the wine cross-stitch motifs within the ribbon pattern. If you would prefer not to work the skip tent stitch on the outside edges, it will in fact resemble the original piece much more closely.

The design has been worked most successfully in a number of colourways, including water-ice pastels on a white canvas. When choosing any colour scheme, it is generally most satisfactory to select colours from one of three ranges: primaries, such as black, red, green, blue and yellow; faded or earth shades (as this one), such as olives, biscuits, terracottas, flame reds, dull and mid-blues; and water-ice pastels, including clear pinks, grass green, sky blues and primrose yellow.

When making up this design it is important to consider that a surround, or better still, a surround and flange as shown here, will set off the points of the lace-like edge to advantage.

RIGHT The lace-like patterns adorning this cushion were particularly popular during the mid-1850s with many variations appearing in canvaswork samples of the period.

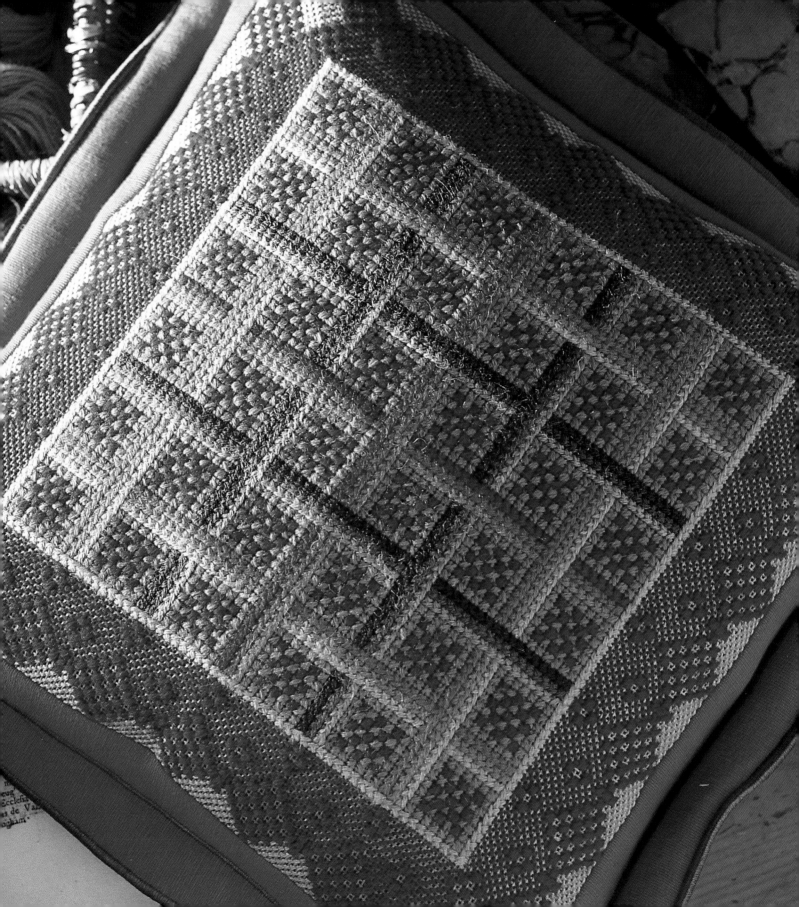

COLOUR KEY

	ACW
	204
	206
	208
	241
	243
	245
	763
	716
	764
	152
	155
	156
	761

ABILITY LEVEL
Intermediate

FINISHED SIZE
30 x 30cm/12 x 12in

THREAD/QUANTITIES
Appleton's Crewel Wool

Colour	No	Small skeins
Mid-blue	152	1
	155	1
	156	1
Flame	204	1
	206	1
	208	1
Olive	241	1
	243	1
	245	1
Biscuit	761	½ hank
	763	½ hank
	764	½ hank
Wine	716	½ hank

NEEDLE SIZE 20

CANVAS
14-mesh in brown

STITCHES
Cross, long-legged cross, mosaic, skip tent

WORKING THE DESIGN
1 Use 3-ply wool throughout, except for skip and reversed skip tent (see page 21) stitches, which are worked with only 2-ply.

2 Mark one edge of the canvas "TOP", keeping the selvedge (if there is one) to the left- or right-hand side. Find the middle by folding and mark with a very small pencil cross. Then mount the canvas on a frame.

2 Measure 7.5cm/3in up from the central cross and just over 10cm/4in out to the left; this will take you to the left-hand starting point for the top of the top horizontal ribbon.

3 Following the chart, use 764 and work 17 full long-legged cross stitches, miss 6 canvas threads (for the vertical ribbon) and continue to work 17 more units; miss 6 threads again and work 17 units.

4 Work the row below with 763, with exactly the same spacing. Work a third row as before with 761.

5 Continue to work the ribbons, following the chart and leaving 14 clear canvas threads in between each ribbon. The gaps come in alternate positions in alternate rows, so proceed carefully. You may prefer to work all horizontal ribbons first, and possibly quarter-turn the canvas to work the vertical ones. Whatever order the ribbons are worked in, it is definitely easier to work the top colour first, then the second and

then the third – as described with the first ribbon.

6 Now work the motifs within the interlacing ribbons, in cross stitch, in 716.

BORDER
7 Work the circuit of long-legged cross stitch (see border) in 716. Working the little four cross-stitch shapes as you go around is neater than working them later. Trail the threads behind the canvas as little as possible as they may show through the finished work.

8 When this is complete work the skip and reversed skip stitches.

9 Infill the cross-stitch motifs between the ribbons with mosaic stitch, in 763.

ALTERNATIVE COLOURWAY

Colour	No	Skeins
Pastel yellow	872	1
Heraldic	841	1
Bright yellow	551	1
Hyacinth	891	1
Hyacinth	892	1
Pastel	877	1
Flamingo	621	1
Flamingo	622	1
Pastel green	873	1
Pastel green	874	1
Bright china blue	741	1

Tulip cushion

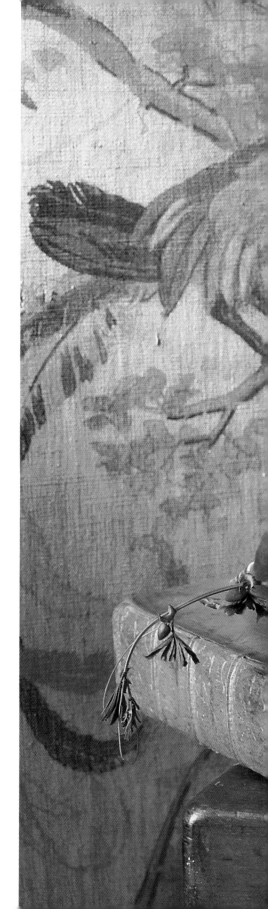

Flowers have always been a favourite with embroiderers. In the 16th century, the flowers were very stiff and stylized, and by the 17th century individual flower sprigs were often worked in tent stitch as slips (see page 9). The original flowers and plants were frequently copied from a book such as *Gerard's Herball*, a well-known publication of the time. Tulips became extremely fashionable. Special "tulipiere" pagoda-shaped vases, with nozzles to hold the flowers at the corners of each storey, were produced in Delft, Holland, in the late 17th century.

This cushion front is adapted from a pattern worked in silks, on a long runner. Its original purpose is a mystery, as above and below the tulip, in half-circles, are part of a rose pattern (sadly not the whole plant). These roses are facing outward, one up and one down, so it is unlikely that the piece was used originally for a pelmet (valance) or part of a bed-hanging. It makes more sense that it was used as a runner for the middle of a table, where people would view it from both sides. The original is softly faded by time and some of the silk has perished, and is in very much the same colours as those suggested for this project. Here, and on the cord and tassels, stranded cotton has been used to give it some lustre.

RIGHT AND ABOVE This cushion was based on part of a long runner. The tassels have been attached only to the outer cord edging the canvas.

ABILITY LEVEL Easy

FINISHED SIZE
33 x 28cm/13 x 11in

THREAD/QUANTITIES
Appleton's Crewel Wool &
DMC Stranded Cotton

APPLETON'S CREWEL WOOL

Colour	No	Skeins
Flame	208	1 small

DMC STRANDED COTTON

Colour	No	Skeins
Beige	842	10
Chocolate	841	12
Terracotta	355	10
Terracotta	356	8

NEEDLE SIZE 22

CANVAS 18-mesh

STITCHES
Florentine, straight gobelin, Victorian
pattern darning

NOTE: We have charted half of the
design on the previous page. Simply
repeat the design in the second half.

WORKING THE DESIGN
1 Use the following plies and
threads:
• 9-ply stranded cotton for
Florentine (Bargello).
• 6-ply stranded cotton for Victorian
pattern darning.
• 3-ply crewel wool for under
straight gobelin stitching.

[NB. On the chart there are three
shades of chocolate/beige shown,
and there are only two reference
numbers given in the quantities list.
In order to get close shading, which
looks particularly attractive with

Florentine, it is necessary to mix the
842 and the 841 stranded cotton in
the needle at the same time – 4 ply
of one and 5 ply of the other.]

2 Find the middle and mark, with a
pencil, through the middle and right
out to the edges of canvas. Then
mount the canvas on a frame.

TULIP
3 Centre the tulip on the canvas,
and work the outline to the tulip
plant. Each stitch is over four canvas
threads and the jump between
stitches is two canvas threads. Use
the darkest terracotta (355), then
work the shadow lines inside the
outline in 356, as shown on the
chart opposite.

4 Infill the flower petals and stems
of the plant.

BORDER
5 Work from the inside edge of the
border out, all stitches over four
canvas threads. Start at the central
bottom point, 16 canvas threads
below the bottom of the tulip stem.
Follow the colours on the chart.

6 For the final border, lay a length
of 3-ply wool along the edge of the
design and work straight gobelin
over the wool on all four sides.

BACKGROUND TO TULIP PLANT
7 Work Victorian pattern darning 1,
with 6-ply 841, vertically up and
down the canvas.

HANDMADE CORD AND TASSELS
The basics are explained on page 18.
The tassels on this cushion have been
done this way, with the mini-tassels
made from uncut stranded cotton,
but when running a thread through

the loop to gather the head, make
it quite long. Next make the cord
using the same colours and thread.
Attach the cord to the cushion and
finally attach each tassel to the cord
with a sharp needle and the long
loop you left to make a few stitches
to secure them at regular intervals.
When secure, bury the thread
back into the tassel and trim. We
originally attached them to the edge
of the cushion and then realised that
mounting them next to the canvas so
that they were supported by the
velvet was more attractive.

**MIXING COLOURS FOR
SPECIAL EFFECTS**
You may not have mixed different
coloured threads in the same needle
before, but with any divisible wool
such as crewel, Medici or stranded
cotton it can extend your colour
palette tremendously. The technique
is most useful for Florentine patterns
and shading. Florentine patterns
become far more sophisticated the
more shades you introduce; an
almost imperceptible change in
colour creates a wonderfully mellow
look. Skies and water are never one
colour and, here, each needle need
not have the same mix as the
previous one. As a general rule, mix
colours next to each other on the
shade card (as here the stranded
cottons 842 and 841). Mixing two
"different" colours may result in an
unpleasant "tweedy" look.

COLOUR KEY

	DMC
	841
	355
	356
	842/841
	842

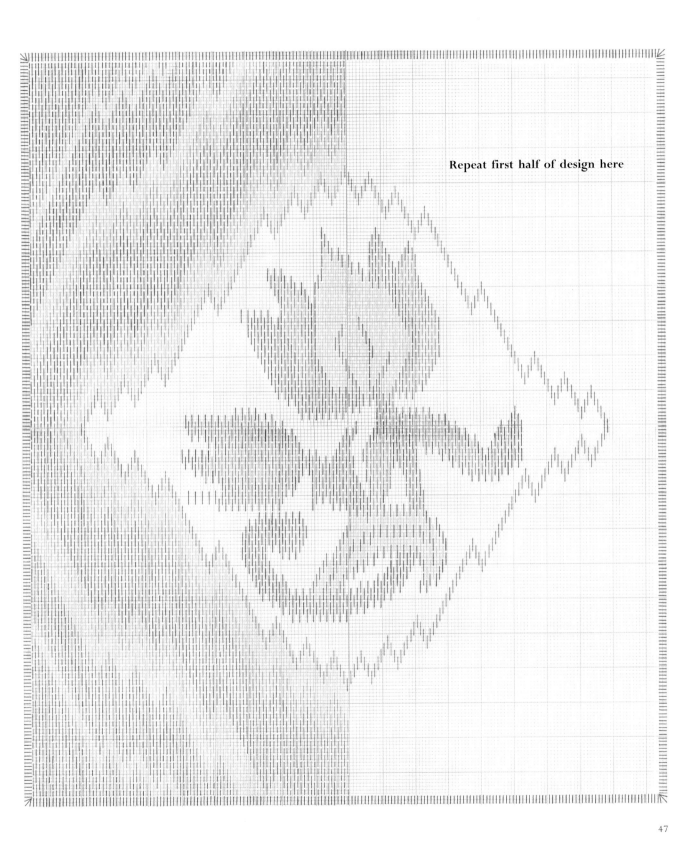

Repeat first half of design here

Pictures
&
Samplers

Delft panel

In the 18th century, the uses for needlework changed and samplers, pictures and more decorative pieces became popular. Needlepoint upholstery suffered a decline in popularity as furniture became lighter and more delicate in structure. Chairs owned by the rich were decorated with distressed paint and gilding, or were made from blond fruitwoods which looked better upholstered in silk damasks rather than needlepoint. Also, the wealthy started to change their interior decor more frequently. Looking at the manufacturers' sample books, it appears that it was common and good business to change their patterns every year – so woven fabrics were more suitable.

This remarkably contemporary-looking piece is dated 1715 by its stitcher, whose initials, E.C., appear in the centre-top of the design. The picture is particularly interesting as the porcelain depicted was only made in the reign of the Chinese emperor, K'ang Hsi (1662–1722). It was this pottery, imported by the Dutch East India Company, that started the vogue for blue and white china in Europe. In the mid-17th century, Delft in Holland became the most important European centre for good-quality tin-glazed earthenware pottery – although its name was often applied to similar wares produced elsewhere in Northern Europe, such as Bristol in England.

The overall design is very pleasing, with a teapot surrounded by pairs of vases and ginger jars decorated with prunus blossom. It is thought that in China these jars were filled with sweetmeats, ginger and tea, given as new year gifts and returned when empty.

The playing cards in the background, while modern, allude to an ever-popular pastime.

RIGHT Although appearing to be very contemporary this picture, featuring vases and ginger jars actually dates back to 1715.

Ability level
Intermediate

Finished size
29 x 33cm/11½ x 13in

Thread
Appleton's Crewel Wool

Needle size
20

Canvas
14-mesh in antique/brown

Stitches
Tent

Working the design
Follow the chart and colours indicated.

NB. The chart shown here is accurate according to the original piece. However, the pieces on either side of the central tea pot and large vase are not, in fact, exact pairs, nor are they on the same line (canvas thread) – so you may prefer to line them up and stitch them as exact copies.

* There is a five-line overlap on each side of the centre of the chart.

Colour key

	ACW
	992
	947
	311
	693
	588
	568
	565
	562

Overlap of 5 lines

Overlap of 5 lines

Berlin woolwork cat

This charming cat comes from a Victorian hand-coloured chart, and is an example of a type of needlepoint that became known as Berlin woolwork.

This type of stitching was developed in the early 19th century by an enterprising print-seller in Berlin whose wife was an accomplished needlewoman. The charts, drawn on point paper (now called graph paper), were specifically designed to be worked in Berlin wool, which was available in many shades and filled the holes in canvas well.

The designs and technique rapidly became a craze throughout England and America, but gradually, as the fashion for it developed into an epidemic, the designs deteriorated. Many thousands of patterns were sold but by the 1850s, when aniline dyes were introduced, flower designs were no longer pretty but voluptuous and exotic; subjects became sentimental, colours were crude, with arsenic-green and magenta much in evidence. Later still, "plushwork" became the rage – designs mostly of flowers and birds worked in loops over a "gauge" (to regulate the length of each loop) giving a high relief. These were then trimmed to give a dense velvety appearance.

This cat, sitting on a red velvet cushion with tassels in each corner, could reflect many things – in an era when animals did not necessarily enjoy the privileges enjoyed by pets of today, this one may have been an extremely good mouser. Alternatively, perhaps this design merely reflects the sentimental aspect of many Berlin patterns.

RIGHT This design, which is from a Victorian hand-coloured chart, is an example of Berlin woolwork, a type of needlepoint which became very popular during the 19th century.

ABILITY LEVEL
Easy

FINISHED SIZE
15.5 x 15.5cm/6 x 6in on 18-mesh
canvas; 21 x 21cm/8 x 8in on
14-mesh canvas

THREAD
Appleton's Crewel Wool

[Quantities: 1 small skein for each
colour]

NEEDLE SIZE
20 for 14-mesh; 22 for 18-mesh

CANVAS
14- or 18-mesh

STITCHES
Tent

WORKING THE DESIGN
Follow the chart and colours
indicated.

FRAMING NEEDLEPOINT
Framing pictures such as the
Berlin Woolwork Cat here or
the Delft Panel (on page 50) is
most probably best left to the
professional. However, there is a
great deal that you can do, right
from the planning stage, to ensure
the best results and to keep the
cost reasonable.

[This is the one instance when it is
best to bind the cut edges of the
canvas with a cloth binding rather
than masking tape.]

1 Block the piece as usual. With a
large piece of work (such as the
Delft Panel), it is best to stretch the
piece on artist stretcher bars. With
a smaller piece, such as this cat

picture, a firm piece of timber or
very strong cardboard is sufficient.

2 Purchase (for the large pieces) four
artist's stretcher bars to form a
frame which will be the same size
as the finished design.

3 Cover this frame with a natural
cotton or linen cover. Choose light
fabric for a pastel design and dark
fabric for a darker one. It may also
be necessary to lay a piece of cotton
wadding/batting or interlining on
top of the cover if there are loose
ends of metallics at the back of the
work to absorb the knots and lumps.

4 Fold the excess canvas over the
edges of the frame (do not trim
the bound canvas). Lace it tightly
with strong fine string from top
to bottom, sewing into the cloth
binding, or just inside it. Fold in
the corners and hold with a
few stitches.

5 Now complete the lacing, working
from side to side.

6 With a small piece, the principle
of folding the unworked canvas to
the back of a board and lacing it is
the same. It will look much better
if the board is covered with some
batting or interlining to absorb any
thread knots or ends.

7 Now the piece can be handed over
to the framer and a decorative frame
can be chosen.

NB. Covering the work with glass
is a personal choice. I think
needlework looks better unglazed.
However, you should not use non-
reflective glass.

COLOUR KEY

	ACW
	993
	964
	323
	921
	120
	500
	947
	945
	400
	620
	477
	300
	552
	690
	240
	540
	830
	960
	460
	450
	800

Country bouquet

The original floral picture shown here was worked in beads on perforated paper. It would have been worked from exactly the same type of Berlin woolwork chart as the cat on page 55. Then, as now, the needleworker would be able to choose what medium to work in: wool and tent stitch, cross stitch (which would have made the piece twice as large), or even beads. As with the other pieces using tent stitch in this book, each stitch (or bead) is represented as a dash in the correct colour. So, whatever materials and stitches are used, the chart can be followed in the same way. Incorporating beads, or indeed working complete designs with beads, was yet another stage which developed in the fashion for Berlin woolwork. Frequently, however, the beads have disappeared on pieces that have otherwise survived.

Berlin canvas, which was made of silk in 21, 29, 34 and 40 threads to the inch (about 8, 11, 13 and 16 threads to the centimetre), was available in many different colours to give the embroideress the option of leaving the background unworked. In this case, the design was worked on perforated paper, a ground only suitable for pictures or items that receive little handling.

Coloured canvases are beginning to appear again, mainly in America. If you are planning unworked areas of canvas in a design they can give a very pleasant effect. It is also now possible to purchase perforated paper, but the embossed designs from the past that you may see in books and embroidery collections – items such as bookmarks, particularly for prayer books and needlecases – do not seem to be available.

RIGHT This piece was originally worked with beads and not wool. If you wish to use beads on a canvaswork piece, sew each bead individually with a tent stitch, using strong thread coated with beeswax.

Overlap of 5 lines

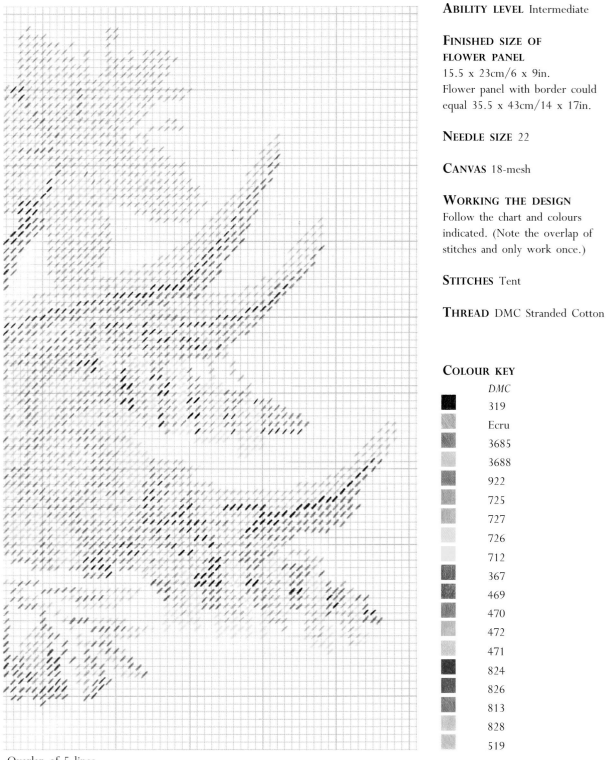

Overlap of 5 lines

ABILITY LEVEL Intermediate

**FINISHED SIZE OF
FLOWER PANEL**
15.5 x 23cm/6 x 9in.
Flower panel with border could
equal 35.5 x 43cm/14 x 17in.

NEEDLE SIZE 22

CANVAS 18-mesh

WORKING THE DESIGN
Follow the chart and colours
indicated. (Note the overlap of
stitches and only work once.)

STITCHES Tent

THREAD DMC Stranded Cotton

COLOUR KEY

	DMC
	319
	Ecru
	3685
	3688
	922
	725
	727
	726
	712
	367
	469
	470
	472
	471
	824
	826
	813
	828
	519

Stitch sampler

This piece is a sampler of stitches and techniques that Victorian needlewomen would have enjoyed making. The long narrow shape makes it an attractive wall-hanging or bell pull.

The earliest known English sampler is dated 1598 and was worked by a Jane Bostocke. By the 19th century, examples come from young ladies' academies, where needlework, music and drawing were considered substantially more important than mathematics and other more traditionally "academic" subjects. Early 17th-century samplers were long, narrow and stitched as a record of motifs rather than a decorative piece; but the typical shape soon changed into a squarer one and the subjects became more pictorial – a building, some flowers and frequently a pious verse were included.

By the end of the 18th century, map samplers were popular: the girls were taught geography at the same time as stitching. If a sampler is not dated, the designs and motifs are the most positive way of dating a piece. In the 17th century, there was a highly defined path that the young girl would follow. Her first sampler would be the reference piece already mentioned, while the second would probably have contained whitework or drawn- and pulled-thread stitches. A more advanced piece often contained raised work, also known as stumpwork, with a box-top panel with figures raised by means of small wooden moulds, frequently representing biblical scenes but sometimes had characters dressed as royalty, such as King Charles II and his wife Catherine of Braganza.

RIGHT This sampler continues the theme of working small motifs and practice stitches. Some of the motifs are taken from the Mary Dowell piece.

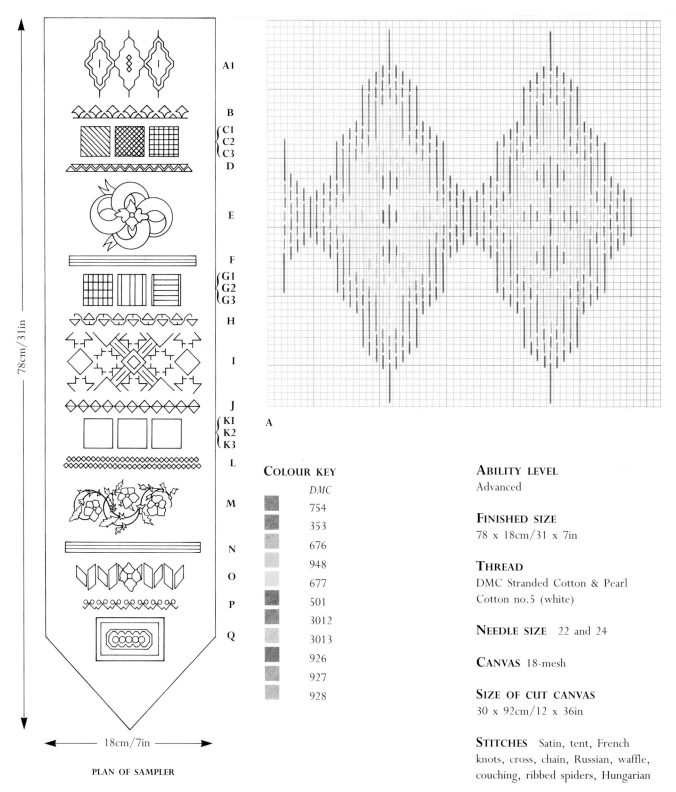

A1
B
C1
C2
C3
D
E
F
G1
G2
G3
H
I
J
KI
K2
K3
L
M
N
O
P
Q

78cm/31in

18cm/7in

PLAN OF SAMPLER

A

COLOUR KEY

	DMC
	754
	353
	676
	948
	677
	501
	3012
	3013
	926
	927
	928

ABILITY LEVEL
Advanced

FINISHED SIZE
78 x 18cm/31 x 7in

THREAD
DMC Stranded Cotton & Pearl
Cotton no.5 (white)

NEEDLE SIZE 22 and 24

CANVAS 18-mesh

SIZE OF CUT CANVAS
30 x 92cm/12 x 36in

STITCHES Satin, tent, French
knots, cross, chain, Russian, waffle,
couching, ribbed spiders, Hungarian

DMC STRANDED COTTON		
Colours	*No*	*Skeins*
Pinks	352	1
	353	1
	754	2
	948	1
Greens	3012	3
	3013	4
Yellows	676	2
	677	2
Blues	501	3
	926	2
	927	1
	928	3
Black		1

PEARL COTTON NO. 5		
Colours	*No*	*Skeins*
White	–	½

WORKING THE DESIGN

1 Carefully mark the top edge of the canvas with "TOP", to avoid later confusion.

2 Start at the bottom, 15cm/6in up, marking threads in the margin only:
33, 7, 7, 36, 8, 57, 10, 6, 24, 6, 8, 6, 46, 5, 10, 5, 24, 6, 8, 68, 5, 6, 24, 6, 10, 6.

Then fold the canvas in half lengthways and baste a cream-coloured thread centrally down the length of the piece.

BORDERS

The centre thread or hole is marked in each diagram and the patterns are numbered from the top. For each of these, used the two shades of green: 3012 and 3013.

Trees (B)

Use 4-ply and tent stitch for this design. There are three hills and three trees either side of the central tree, which makes seven trees and six hills in all.

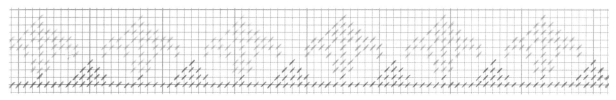

B

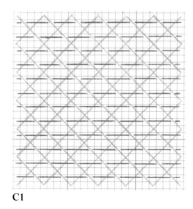

C1

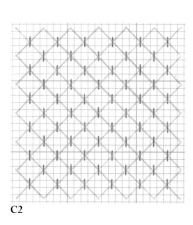

C2

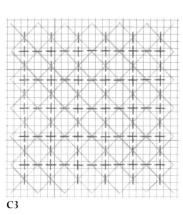

C3

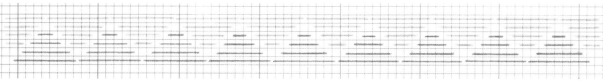

D

Triangles (D)

Use 6-ply thread. There are stitches over 8, 6, 4 and 2 canvas threads, and note that the stitches over 8 threads share a hole. There are 6 dark triangles either side of the centre, making 13 in all and 12 light ones.

Sheaves (F)

Use 6-ply for first stage; 4-ply for lacing. Work 4 upright stitches over 8 threads and tie this group with a central horizontal stitch (in line at both ends as in the diagram). There are 26 sheaves, and both ends of the row will line up with the triangle pattern (D) and the berry pattern (H).

When the row is complete, use 4-ply dark green and lace through the horizontal bars forward, back and forward. There will be two loops above and one loop below alternately, as shown in the chart.

Berries (H)

Use 4-ply. There are four berries either side of the central one, making nine in all.

Eggs in a basket (J)

Use 6-ply. Baskets (darker green) are over 10, 8, 6, 4, 2 and all the eggs are over 2 threads. This pattern is slightly longer than the berries above.

Double diamonds (L)

Use 4-ply. There are 28 dark diamonds and 27 light diamonds. The light diamond pattern lines up with the eggs in a basket on the left and it is one thread in on the right.

Upright satin (N)

Use 6-ply. The pairs of stitches are over 5 and 2 threads; there are 27 pairs of tall stitches. The dark finishes with a pair over 2 threads each end, and the light with a pair over 5 threads each end. This pattern lines up with the light green in the double diamond pattern above it (see plan on page 64).

Bows (P)

Use 4-ply. There are 7 bows (shorter than the borders above) and only six are shown here.

DAMASK STITCHES (G1, 2, 3)

Use 6-ply in both shades of blue, 926 and 928.

COLOUR KEY

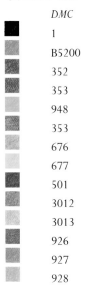

	DMC
	1
	B5200
	352
	353
	948
	353
	676
	677
	501
	3012
	3013
	926
	927
	928

E

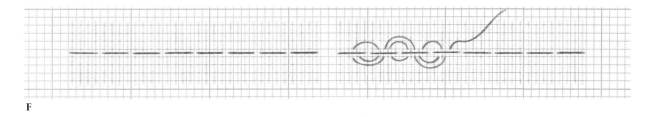

F

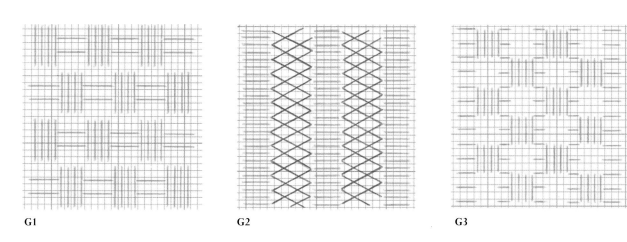

G1

G2

G3

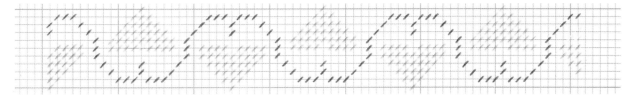

H

Central panel (G2)

Work 3 rows of horizontal satin stitches over 4 canvas threads, leaving 6 threads bare between the rows. When complete, work the Russian stitch (see stitch diagram in *Before you begin*). Start at the top of the column.

Left panel (G1)

Use 6-ply lighter blue (928). Work in horizontal rows, from the lower right-hand corner. Leave 5 bare threads from the

bottom left corner of the central panel already worked (as the horizontal stitches in the second row of this panel cover one more thread). Work groups of 4 vertical stitches over 6 threads, then two horizontal stitches over 5 threads (stitch from left to right so that you can tuck under the vertical stitches); then a vertical group followed by horizontal stitches, etc. In the second and subsequent rows, the vertical stitches are above the horizontal, and the horizontal are above the vertical.

Right panel (G3)

Use 6-ply of the lighter blue (628) thread. First set up vertical columns of horizontal stitches. Start on the left-hand side, leaving only 4 threads of canvas bare between the central panel and this one. Note that the two outer columns are over 3 canvas threads and the inner columns are over two threads only. Then, starting in the upper left, work groups of 4 stitches over 4 threads diagonally across the canvas.

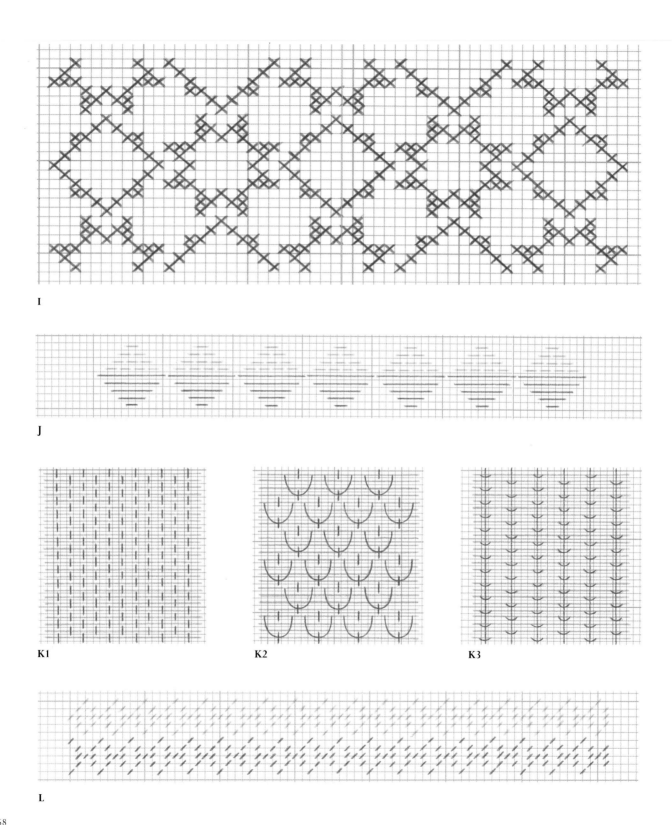

I

J

K1

K2

K3

L

M

Colour key

	ACW
■	501
■	3012
■	3013
■	926
■	928

Panel banks

These are the three banks of stitches. Use the two blues, 926 and 928. In each bank it is suggested that you start with the central panel, positioning it centrally on the basting line stitched on the canvas. Each panel is 24 threads square and there are 4 bare canvas threads between them.

Open laid fillings (C1, C2, C3)

Using 6-ply of the lighter blue (928) thread to set up the trellis for each of the panels, make long diagonal stitches first from upper left to lower right, and then from upper right to lower left, as in the chart on page 65. The trellis for the middle and right panels should be interlaced, not the trellis for the left panel.

Central panel (C2)

When the trellis is complete, use 6-ply of the darker blue thread (926) and run up and down the vertical rows over 2 threads and under 2 threads. The second and subsequent rows are staggered, as shown in the diagram.

Left panel (C1)

When the trellis is complete, use 2-ply 926 and weave horizontal rows on the surface, without entering the canvas. Only take the needle and thread down through the canvas at the end of each line.

Right panel (C3)

When the trellis is complete, use 2-ply and first backstitch over 2 threads in horizontal rows so the rows are 4 threads apart. When the horizontal rows are complete, backstitch again in vertical rows, again with 4 threads between rows.

Couching (K1, K2, K3)

In each panel lie 6-ply of the lighter blue (928) across the 24-thread panel with a long stitch behind the work, to help hold the correct tension. Couch each row as laid, except when told differently below.

Central panel (K2)

Use 6-ply light blue; 4-ply darker. Work from the top down. Centre this panel on the "Eggs in the basket" that is immediately above, and start seven threads down. First row: lay the lighter blue across the 24 threads left to right, and bring it up at the left-hand end ready to lay the second row; take the dark blue and couch the first row every sixth hole (there will be three stitches). Lay the 2nd, 3rd and 4th lighter blue rows and couch down following the couching diagram (see page 23 in *Before You Begin*).

Left panel (K1)

Again, use 6-ply lighter and 4-ply darker blue. Start at the top of the area, and lay a light blue thread

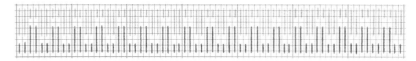

N

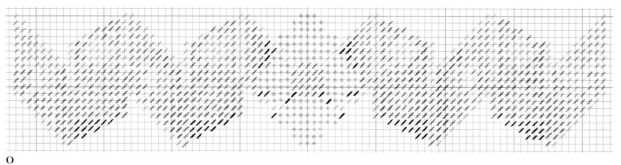

O

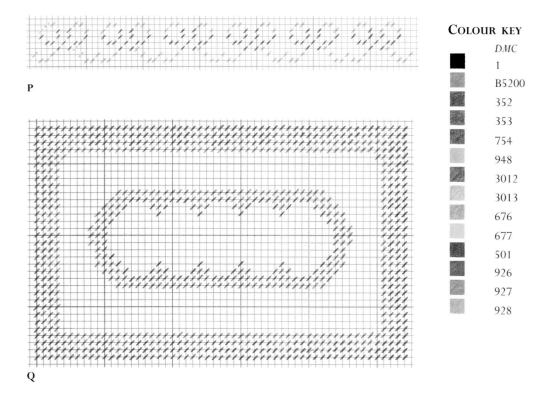

P

Q

Colour key

	DMC
■	1
	B5200
	352
	353
	754
	948
	3012
	3013
	676
	677
	501
	926
	927
	928

from side to side and couch with small vertical stitches over 2 threads in darker blue. Leave 4 threads between vertical stitches. Work only 23 laid threads. The vertical stitches are staggered on second and subsequent rows; it is easier to come up at the bottom of the stitch, go over the thread to be couched and tuck under the thread above with the point of the needle.

Right panel (K3)

Again, use 6-ply lighter thread and 4-ply darker thread. Lay all 23 horizontal rows of the lighter blue. With the darker blue, work vertical stitches every 4 threads (starting 2 threads in from the left-hand edge) from top to bottom of the area. Use the darker blue thread to work a horizontal row, crossing the 1st, 3rd, 5th etc. vertical stitch immediately under the top horizontal row. On the next row, cross the second, fourth, sixth stitch etc. The third row will be the same as the first and the fourth as the second.

DECORATIVE MOTIFS

Triple Florentine (A)

Use 9-ply throughout. This motif is at the top, starting 6 canvas threads above the top of the trees. The chart shows the central lozenge and the one to the right. The colour scheme for the right and the left ones are identical. All outlines are 501; follow the chart for the other colours.

Flower Posy (E)

Situated between triangles (D) and sheaves (F). All in tent stitch

except the white French knots. Use 6-ply stranded cotton and 1-ply pearl cotton.

Star and Diamond Paving Pattern (I)

Use 6-ply darkest blue 501, and cross stitch. Waffle and Hungarian stitches are worked in the central diamond. Use 6-ply 353 for the diagonal stitches and 352 for Hungarian. (See page 22 in *Before You Begin* for stitch diagram and description.)

Ribbed spiders should be worked in the two star shapes either side of central diamond. Use 6-ply 353, with quite a long length, as the thread cannot be changed during weaving. Set up the spokes going down into the centre. Bring up the needle between two spokes and weave on the surface back over one spoke, forward under two — then continue until all the spokes are tightly packed.

Spaced diagonal Florence: (See page 23 in the *Before You Begin section*). Turn the chart around to match the area to be worked). Use 6-ply 677.

Pansies (M)

Follow the template (actual size) on page 69 to help you stitch; use long and short stitch. This stitch (also known as brick stitch) is a filling stitch, worked similarly to satin stitch, but with stitches of varied lengths, producing a broken-textured feather stitch.

Use 3-ply throughout and a size 24 needle. Outline the petals first using split stitch (a stitch similar to stem stitch, but the thread is split half-

way along the stitch), taking care to cover all the outlines, then work long and short stitches.

Work the stems in chain stitch (see page 22 in the *Before You Begin* section).

FLOWER BAND (O)

Use 6-ply and the same colours as the Flower Posy.

RECTANGULAR PANEL (Q)

Complete the frame following the chart and then use 6-ply thread to stitch the initials or date of your choice.

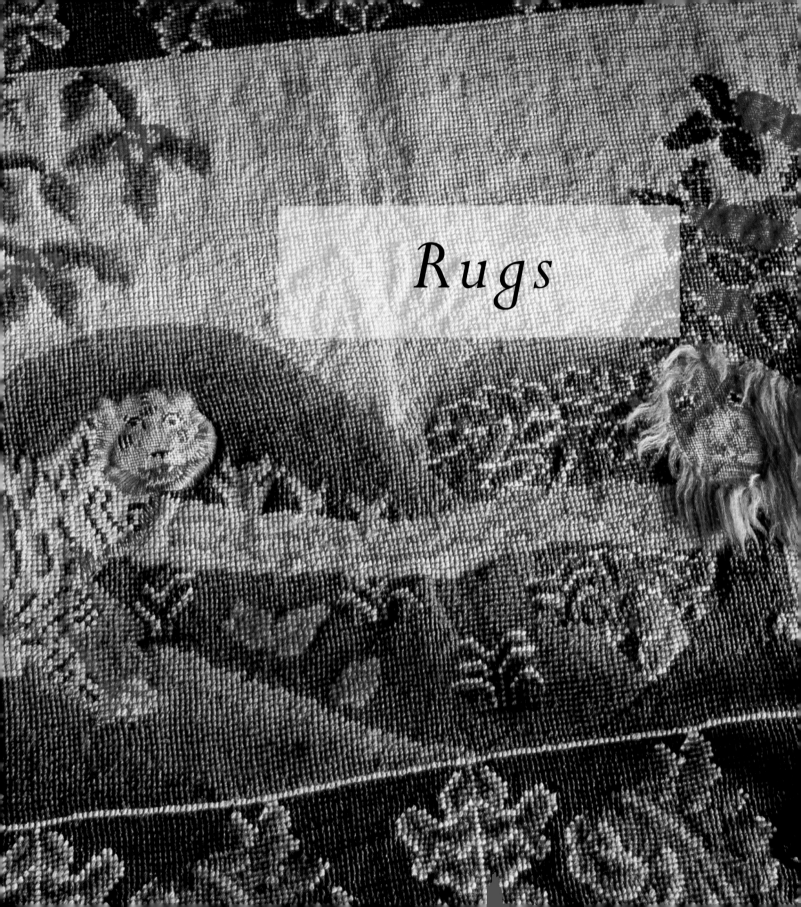

Rugs

Miniature rug

The original, full-sized carpet on which this miniature rug has been based can be found in the Music Room at Harewood House in Yorkshire, England.

The present 18th-century exterior of Harewood was designed by John Carr of York, but Robert Adam was responsible for much of the marvellous interior, and this house remains one of his greatest achievements. His mark can be seen in everything from the ceiling to the floor covering, the elaborate decoration of almost any flat surface as well as the plasterwork, decorative panels and, most important of all, the use of furniture by Thomas Chippendale.

The Music Room has undergone little change since Adam's design, and the classical, round ceiling is mirrored by the hand-made Axminster carpet. The musical theme is emphasized everywhere with lyres, pipes and trumpets carved on the marble chimney, ormolu trophies of instruments on the Sèvres clock, and various paintings depicting performing musicians and a group of brigands playing pipes.

A dolls' house miniature is usually worked on the scale of 25mm to 30cm (this is the traditional measurement of 1in to 1ft). When re-scaling a piece, it is necessary to capture the general effect of the design rather than include every detail – unless of course you wish to work on extremely fine silk gauze which is available in 48 threads to 2.5cm (1in). Similarly, the colours of the original, which are still extremely fresh and vibrant, have been somewhat muted here to harmonize with the miniature size.

LEFT Tent stitch is the most suitable stitch for a dolls' house rug, as other more textured stitches are not really in keeping with the miniature theme.

C

C

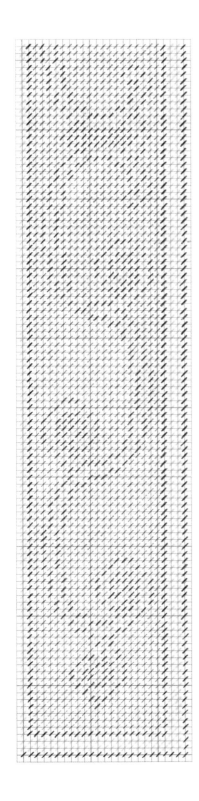

COLOUR KEY

	DMC
	822
	223
	819
	841
	676
	842
	677
	3012
	3013
	932

ABILITY LEVEL
Intermediate

FINISHED SIZE
19 x 25cm/7½ x 10in

[NB. If a square carpet is preferred the borders on the two ends could be left off giving a 19cm/7½in square size]

THREADS/QUANTITIES
DMC Stranded Cotton

Colour	No	Skeins
Honey brown	841	10
Light yellow	677	2
Dark yellow	676	2
Light pink	819	2
Dark pink	223	4
Ecru	—	1
Light brown	842	1
Blue	932	2
Dark green	3012	2
Light green	3013	3

[NB. For honey brown – if no border only 8 skeins needed; for dark pink – 3 skeins if no border]

NEEDLE SIZE 24

CANVAS 24-mesh

WORKING THE DESIGN

1 Use 3 ply of the stranded cotton for this design, making sure that you strip it before use as explained on page 15.

2 Follow the chart and colours, matching the centre of the canvas to the centre of the chart. Work in the lower right quarter first, using the chart to guide you.

3 Work in the lower-right quarter first. Complete this central motif out to the single row of dark olive (3012).

4 Next work both the scallops in old gold (676). Make the second row of scallops into circles with dark olive (3012).

5 Complete both the inner and outer circles of rose (223), and then work the corner motifs as shown. Now work the rose (223) design between the dark olive (step 2) and the inner scallop in old gold.

6 Work the two infills for the circles and then the backgrounds.

7 If the border is to be worked, match the centre of this chart to the centre of the right-hand side of your work and follow the chart working the scrolls first. Copy a mirror image of these scrolls in the upper-right before working any background.

8 Turn this chart or your canvas upside-down. Work the upper left-hand area again by working from the centre up, and then the mirror image down.

Tartan rug

There could not be a greater difference between the fine canvas of the previous project and the large mesh of this rug. This big canvas is tremendous fun to work and the stitching grows incredibly quickly; in fact on the 24-mesh canvas used for the previous piece (miniature rug) there are 576 stitches in each square 25 x 25mm (1 x 1in) and on this 7-mesh canvas there are only 49! In the complete miniature (approximately 20 x 20cm/8 x 8in without the borders) there are over 36,000 stitches, while in this large rug, measuring 97 x 149cm (38 x 55in) there are just over 100,000 stitches – which is slightly over twice the work for a much larger piece.

Tartan patterns can actually be dated back to the time of the Roman Empire. There are district tartans in Ireland, Canada and parts of Britain, and new designs are still being created and registered. In many of the tartans designed for the American and Canadian states, the colours used are symbolic or are taken from flags or an official emblem of a bird or flower.

To work both the horizontal and diagonal tartans on canvas requires a special technique so that the colours weave through each other (see page 22).

RIGHT AND ABOVE If you would prefer an all-over tartan, you need not work the leaf border. However, the inclusion of a border, monogram or some kind of motif makes the tartan look particularly special.

ABILITY LEVEL
Intermediate

FINISHED SIZE
7 x 149cm/38 x 55in

THREADS/QUANTITIES
Appleton's Crewel Wool

Colour	No	Hanks
Peacock	643	10
Peacock	646	18
Wine	716	7
Biscuit	761	12

NEEDLE SIZE   18

CANVAS   7-mesh

STITCHES
Tartan, crossed corner,
long-legged cross

[NB. The panel behind the oak
leaves could be in a one-colour
basketweave tent.]

WORKING THE DESIGN
1 Use 6-ply wool, except where
otherwise stated.

2 Find the middle of the canvas by
folding, and then mark horizontally
and vertically right out the edges of
the canvas.

3 Mount the canvas on a frame to
enable you to work on the central
area. Holding the canvas portrait-
fashion, mark A in upper left and
B in upper right. Quarter-turn the
canvas to the right (12 o'clock to 3
o'clock) and mark C in upper left
and D in upper right (A and D will
be in the same corner).

4 Turn the canvas back to portrait
with AB at the top, and with a
pencil draw the following lines: from
the middle count out and mark 34
threads to the right, then 4, then
36, then 4, then 53, then 4, 4, and
finally 4 threads. Count the same to
the left and mark as before.

5 Cut the wool hanks as you need
them. All the wools, except for
the wine (716), should be cut
once at each end; the wine for
the central tartan area should be
cut into three equal lengths:
when the outer tartan area is
worked, this colour will be cut as all
the rest. When working the outer
tartan area some of the rows are
very long. Avoid starting and
finishing threads in the same area
(in a line) as this may cause a lump
behind the work.

6 The special stitching technique
that creates the colours weaving
through each other is most probably
different to other stitching that you
may have undertaken. Sometimes
it is necessary to count the threads,
sometimes to count stitches.
Follow the particular instruction
exactly. As with all tartan patterns
the number of the horizontal rows
in a colour is exactly the same as
the vertical rows. For ease of
handling the large canvas, on some
occasions it is suggested you
turn the canvas upside-down, a
full half-turn; this is not the same
as changing from the AB position
to the CD position which is a
quarter-turn.

TARTAN RECIPE
1 row highlight: wine 716
2 rows neutral: biscuit 761
2 rows light: peacock 643
1 row highlight: wine 716
5 rows dark: peacock 646

CENTRAL TARTAN PANEL
7 In AB position: Count out 33
threads from the central mark
horizontally to the right. This should
be one thread inside the pencil line.
Leaving a wool tail two inches to
the right, work a row across the
middle, doing a stitch and missing a
stitch; this row will comprise 33
stitches, and it will take you past the
central mark and out equally to the
left, again one thread inside your
pencil mark. Take the end of the
wool out to left on the right side of
the work.

8 Continue working down the canvas
(toward you) following the recipe
(ie. with the first row of biscuit 761
next), with 34 stitches in the second
row (which will involve an extra
stitch at both ends giving a 67-thread
width for the central panel). You
should be able to work the two
rows required with the one length of
wool. Chart 1 shows the first stitch
in the wine, one thread away from
the wine. One thread away from the
crossed corner border.

9 Work the complete recipe six
times plus an additional two more
rows of recipe, ie. one row wine
and one row of biscuit. (Every so
often the tails left at the ends of the
rows can be caught with the crossed
corner stitch border.) Turn upside-
down and work as before, finishing
at the same point. The approximate
size of this area is 22 x 63.5cm/
8¼ x 25in.

10 For the dark line around this
panel, work crossed corners stitch in
dark peacock 646 as a border down
both sides (also shown in chart 1).
This is the way to catch all the
tails of the wool used to stitch the

C

C

Colour key

ACW

716

646

643

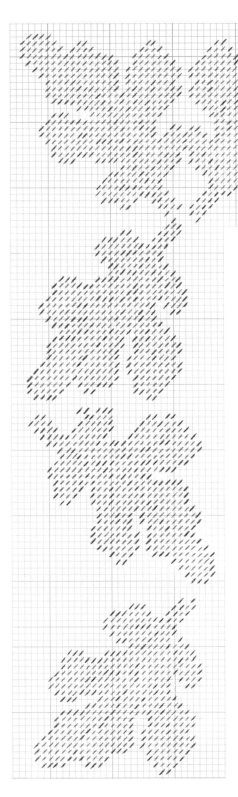

central tartan; they can then be caught back into the crossed corners and trimmed off. Work in chunks, keeping up with but not passing the worked rows of tartan stitches. Don't necessarily work right down to the corners at this stage.

OUTER TARTAN

11 Leave the 36-thread channel bare on both sides and work a second crossed corners row in the four-thread channel as before. Still in the AB position, start the outer tartan panel, carefully matching across from the central highlight row (the first one you stitched) and work a row of 27 stitches, the first sharing a hole with the outer edge of the crossed corners just worked; the last stitch will share with the pencil line.

12 Before moving on, work the highlight row on the opposite side, again 27 stitches long and sharing with the crossed corners border. Besides the final three rows of crossed corners worked around the whole design you now have the full width of the rug. As before, work down, but the second line (on both sides) will be 26 stitches. When a few rows of this area is established

you can return to the central area and complete the CD stitching.

CENTRAL PANEL

13 In CD position, start in the new right-hand corner of the central area, one stitch in from the corner (as there is one there already). Work the recipe from the top row down, starting with 1 row neutral, 1 row highlight, 2 neutral etc., as before. Complete this central area.

14 Complete both the crossed corners borders on all four sides leaving 36 threads bare at the bottom and top, the same as on the sides. There is one crossed corner stitch on each side, only over three threads.

OUTER BORDER

15 Return to the AB position and the outer tartan border. Work down the sides until reaching the lower edge of the inner crossed corners border and work all the way across. This will be the first of two neutral rows. Work 53 long rows in all (also ending on two neutral rows). Turn upside-down and repeat.

16 In CD position: starting at the top in the corner, start the recipe with two biscuit, one wine, two biscuit etc. Work whole area.

OAK-LEAF BORDER

17 In the AB position, follow the chart on this page for the lower right and upper left corners, and the chart on the following page for the upper right and lower left corners. At this stage, if you plan to work the diagonal tartan background, it is better to work only outlines and veins of the leaves with 6-ply 646.

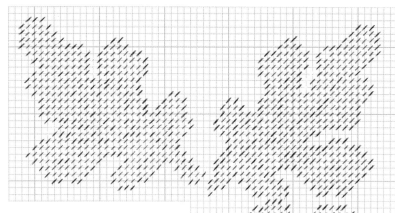

18 For the background to the oak leaves, either basketweave tent in the biscuit 761 can be worked, or use diagonal tartan (as in the photograph). To start diagonal tartan work the recipe as chart 1, starting in the middle of the right-hand long side of the rug. (The count is one peacock 643, two biscuit, one wine, four biscuit, one wine, two biscuit, one peacock 643, etc.) Each row of stitches is on the diagonal, just like basketweave tent; start the first row in the middle of the long right-hand side so it matches up with the chart.

19 Continue the recipe (see page 80) as before, working across small areas of leaves or going around the leaf and matching up the other side (it is now that you will find having left the leaves empty helps you to count accurately across). When the whole area is complete, turn the canvas to the CD position and repeat; the angle of each stitch is different, as shown in the diagram, but the recipe is the same.

INFILL FOR LEAVES

20 Decide which half of each leaf should be dark and which light for the best definition; use 6-ply peacock 643 for the light side and 2-ply peacock 646 plus 4-ply peacock 643 for the darker half.

FINAL BORDER AND FINISHING THE RUG

21 Work three rows of crossed corners. The first and third are completely in peacock 646, the middle row has the base cross in peacock 646 and the four tipping stitches in peacock 643.

22 After working the first row of the crossed corners, allow ten rows

of canvas to show and turn the rest to the back; finger press, lining up canvas threads on both levels. Now stitch the final two rows of crossed corners, colours as above, through both layers of canvas.

23 Finally, using 8-ply of peacock 646, work binding stitch over the two thread edges. To finish, trim the raw canvas away to six threads from the final stitching. Bind with pre-shrunk webbing tape to prevent fraying.

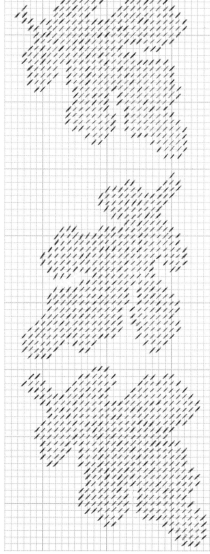

COLOUR KEY

	ACW
	646
	643

Tiger rug

This charming piece was accurately dated when it was sold recently. The vendor said that her great-grandmother had stitched it for her "bottom drawer" prior to her wedding in 1870. Without this information, it could easily be thought to be fifty years older, as many needlewomen of that period copied the popular paintings by George Stubbs showing horses, lions and other animals.

The primitive style would appear to be the stitcher's own design rather than a design prepared by a professional, and it is all the more charming as a result: the decorative trees with their amazing fruit, the lion's den with its interior in a fashionable coral, and the border with stylized leaves worked in cross stitch.

Only the tiger has been charted overleaf. Enlarge the outline drawing and transfer it onto canvas if you wish to replicate the actual piece. The original canvas is 14-mesh, and the central design is worked in tent stitch, except for the lion's mane which is fringed. You could make a handsome pair of cushions, one with the tiger and one with a lion, but it will be necessary to use your imagination where the lion's body is obscured by the tree.

Working out borders to fit a particular design can be very awkward and both the leaves on this rug (and those on the tartan rug) illustrate two ways of solving the problem. The tartan rug only has a group of leaves as a corner motif. Therefore, if you wish to alter the size, the corner motifs would still be worked in each corner but the distance between the groups would be different. Here, each leaf is isolated. Fewer leaves could be worked on a smaller rug or the same number of leaves (with a few more canvas threads between each) could make the border dimensions bigger.

LEFT The tiger and lion design on this charming rug, stitched in the late 19th century, could be easily adapted to make an attractive set of cushions.

COLOUR KEY

	ACW	DMC
■	993	
▨	992	
▨	715	
▨	478	
▨		834
▨	474	
▨	761	
▨	342	

ABILITY LEVEL
Intermediate

FINISHED SIZE OF RUG
145 x 82cm/57 x 32in

FINISHED SIZE OF TIGER ONLY
36 x 26cm/14 x 10in

THREAD FOR TIGER
Appleton's Crewel Wool &
DMC Stranded Cotton

NEEDLE SIZE
20

CANVAS
16 in antique/brown;

14 would also be a good choice and would make the rug slightly larger.

WORKING THE DESIGN
If you would like to work the tiger only, follow the chart and the colours indicated. If the whole piece is to be copied, enlarge the central design (plan given on page 86) and trace it onto the canvas. Only mark the hillocks, tree trunks and branches – not the fine details, as you will probably wish to create your own flowers and fruit.

Work the tiger first, following the chart below. For the the border, use the chart on page 88.

WOOL FRINGE

A heavy wool fringe edges this rug on all four sides. Oriental runners traditionally have fringe only on the two short sides. A fringe should be made with spare wool in one or two of the colours from the design.

To fringe this piece, complete the stitching of the design, stretch the piece, trim the canvas and slipstitch raw canvas to the back of the work. Cut lengths of wool approximately twice as long as you want the fringe (13cm/5in would give a fringe of roughly 6cm/2¼in). Thread both ends of a length through the eye of a needle, so you can pull the ends tight through the loop when stitched. Work from the back of the carpet and insert the needle two canvas threads from the edge, coming out on the

Overlap of 5 lines

edge and through the loop.
Pull the ends tight through the
loop. Repeat on every alternate
threads, depending on how
thick you want the fringe to be.
Slipstitch the backing to the rug
if required.

WALL-HANGINGS

Although this piece was designed
as a rug it would make a wonderful
wall-hanging. In fact, it was hung
as that in the antique shop
who kindly let us photograph
it. Only the final making-up
would differ from that of a rug
or carpet. There are various
alternatives that you should
consider, but in none of them
would a fringe be appropriate.

First, you should decide whether
you want it be be suspended
from a decorative pole or not. A
decorative pole could be brass,

wrought iron or a polished
wood curtain pole with finials
at either end. The needlepoint
could be fixed with loops of
plain co-ordinating fabric or this
same fabric could be used to
surround the design to form
a frame.

HIDDEN FIXING

If you prefer a hidden fixing,
then the most satisfactory method
is to back the piece with closely-
woven linen and, with the
same fabric, make a channel
along the top. Slide it on a
strong wooden or metal rod
mounted to the wall with brackets
which cannot be seen under the
needlework. Do not simply attach
a series of rings that are hung on
a rod, as the weight of the
needlework would pull the piece
down between the rings in a very
unattractive way.

If, after stretching the piece,
you are not particularly confident
that it will remain straight and true,
then mounting the canvas on a
firm board – probably edged with
a plain fabric – would be best.
The thickness of the board would
depend on the size of the work.
It is obvious that the stronger
the board, the better it will hold
the work straight.

When mounting it on the board,
use the same lacing procedure as
for a picture (see page 56). If
the canvas is to be surrounded
with a fabric, machine-stitch a
width of fabric (the width should
be the measurement of what you
wish to be seen as a surround,
plus an additional 5cm/2in) on
all four sides, mitring the corners.
Position the canvas and the
fabric frame on cardboard and
lace as before.

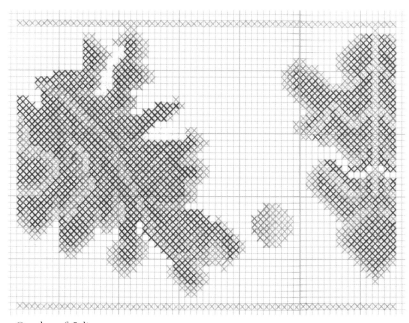
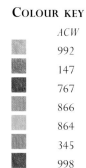

Overlap of 5 lines

COLOUR KEY

	ACW
	992
	147
	767
	866
	864
	345
	998

Furnishings

Victorian chair motif

The design on this chair is particularly pleasing. The scale and balance of the needlepoint seems to complement the shape of the chair very well and the colours of the flowers, especially the *ipomoea* or *convolvulus*, are still quite vibrant. The *ipomoea*, also known as morning glory, has been chosen to chart here as it is not common in needlepoint and the intense blue is so beautiful.

The scroll surrounding the floral design is very well planned, particularly the way that it spreads out on the shoulders of the chair. The best way to undertake a pattern with a mirror image like this is to plot it out first on graph paper.

Alternatively, the design can be drawn and stitched, working a little on one side of the design and a little on the other, balancing stitch by stitch each side as you go along.

Strangers' Hall – the museum in Norwich, England, where this attractive chair is displayed – catalogue it as a *prie-Dieu* chair, used when praying, often in a bedroom. A person knelt on the seat and rested the prayer book on the wide "shelf" formed by the back rail. With *prie-Dieu* chairs, it would be normal for the seat to be even closer to the ground than this one – while the back would be taller in proportion. However, as this example is not so elongated it is just as attractive as a normal chair.

However, recently a French visitor has insisted that this chair has been incorrectly identified as a *prie-Dieu*, but is actually a *chaise de voyeuse*. This type of chair is used at a games table – a spectator could sit back to front and lean on the padded back-rail and watch the popular game of Bezique.

RIGHT Displayed in Strangers' Hall museum in Norwich, England, this chair has a beautiful floral design. The ipomoea is particularly attractive, and is charted on the following pages.

COLOUR KEY

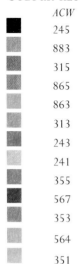

ACW

245

883

315

865

863

313

243

241

355

567

353

564

351

ABILITY LEVEL
Intermediate

FINISHED SIZE
20 x 15cm/8 x 6in

THREAD
Appleton's Crewel Wool

NEEDLE SIZE
20

CANVAS
14-mesh

STITCHES
Tent

WORKING THE DESIGN
Follow the chart and colours
indicated. (Overlap of 5 lines
on each page.)

The chart provided here is for the
ipomoea – the central section of a

Overlap of 5 lines

complex floral design from the
Victorian chair.

There are many different mediums
available to display this design. You
may wish to take this design and use
it on your own chair. If so, you
should take your finished piece of
needlepoint to an upholsterer for a
professional finish.

ADAPTING THE DESIGN
Such a pretty design would be
perfect for a multitude of projects
from small to large. It would make
a very attractive cushion, simply
worked with a few centimetres of
background around it or, if a lager
cushion was needed, the finished
canvas could be mounted on an

Overlap of 5 lines

existing cushion with handmade cord or plait (see page 18) to mask the edges.

For a particularly attractive result, take two cords, one quite thin and another thicker, and attach them to the edge of the canvas (in the same colour scheme) and to edge the cushion itself. By making this cord a little longer than necessary, small twirls can be formed and stitched into place in each corner. Consider one of the lacy pattern darning stitches or skip tent as a background rather than the more solid-looking basketweave – especially if the finished piece is not going to receive a much wear.

BORDERS

A border would be another way of making a larger design. It could be a variation of the florentine worked around the tulips (on page 46), or the Florentine cushion (page 33).

Even when buying canvas for a simple project such as a cushion, be generous with the size; as already recommended, 5cm/2in left unworked on all sides is essential for the stretching and making up process. However, unless you are absolutely sure that you do not want a border or already know the exact width of the border you will work, take plenty of material. Nothing is more frustrating than only having enough canvas to work a narrow edging when a really magnificent design has presented itself to you.

Pole firescreen

Large, decorative firescreens are frequently used to fill empty fireplaces during the summer, or at other times when the fire is not lit. Although they often constitute a sizeable piece of needlepoint (about 46 x 76cm/18 x 30in) they can look extremely smart if the right design is chosen. A coat of arms or, if you have connections with a Scottish clan, the clan badge superimposed on the correct tartan would be very dramatic.

This particular design (the large rose in the lower-right has been charted here) is worked in fine tent stitch to a Berlin woolwork pattern. When considering a project such as a screen, which will get very little wear from handling or being sat or walked upon, every sort of stitch and thread can be considered. Embroidery stitches such as long and short, French knots, couching and silk or metallic threads can all look good if used in the right way.

You may even consider leaving the background bare as the needleworker did in this instance, or possibly working it in one of the Victorian pattern darning designs that are illustrated on page 21. Alternatively, the design would make a charming pincushion (on 18-mesh), or a small cushion front (on 14- or even coarser mesh).

One reason why this pole screen is so attractive is because of the beautifully shaped mount. Leaving the background unworked would have looked decidedly unfinished here without the gentle curves of the mount surrounding and "holding" the flower posy so well. Also, the thickness of the mounting card is crucial, as it is most important that the glass does not touch the stitching. A really thick mount helps keep the glass well away.

RIGHT Pole firescreens such as this were used in the 18th and 19th centuries to shield the face from the heat of the fire, as a ruddy complexion was not admired. The height could be adjusted by moving it up and down on the pole.

COLOUR KEY

	ACW
■	998
■	948
■	754
■	311
■	245
■	312
■	241
■	243

ABILITY LEVEL
Beginner

FINISHED SIZE
18 x 18 cm/7 x 7in on
14-mesh canvas

THREAD
Appleton's Crewel Wool

Colour	No	Skeins
Charcoal	998	1
Pink	754	1
	948	1
Green	241	1
	243	1
	245	1
Olive	311	1
	312	1

NEEDLE SIZE
22 (for 18-mesh)
20 (for 14-mesh)

CANVAS
14- or 18-mesh

STITCHES
Tent

WORKING THE DESIGN
Follow the chart and colours
as indicated.

ADAPTING THE DESIGN
The rose motif, taken from the
antique pole firescreen, would
make a lovely design for
something circular – such as a
footstool, pincushion or hexagonal
cushion. Be generous with the
piece of canvas that you work on,
and always work any design on
square or rectangular pieces of
canvas so that they will fit tautly
onto the frame. They should be
trimmed to the right shape only
after they are finished.

Another important tip – useful
for any design where you might
decide to work a border, square,
round or hexagonal – is to mark
the centre of the canvas with a
very small cross and then the central
point on all four edges. Do not
mark all the way out in case you
select a lacy stitch for the
background which would not cover
your guide marks. These central
marks will make it much easier to
count any border.

CIRCLES
To create a circle, draw a circular
shape very lightly with an HB
pencil, making sure that you miss
all the outer leaves, tendrils or
design elements of the central
motif. Working again with two
needles, and starting in the same
way as with the hexagon, work
groups of continental tent stitch
following the faint line on the
canvas as closely as possible.
Work groups of stitches in
decreasing numerical order – for
example, 8,6,4,2,2,2,1,1,1.

FLORAL DESIGNS
It seems that flowers have always
been popular with needleworkers.
Elizabethan ladies loved stylized
interpretations, Jacobean
embroiderers stitched flowers in
a very free-flowing way and
Victorians, as we have seen,
slavishly copied the fashion for
cottage garden roses, morning glory,
daisies and bluebells; in the later
period, it was the exotic hot-house
orchids and lilies. For this reason,
I have included a number of flower
and leaf designs which you can
choose to copy or adapt, but you
could also copy a favourite
wallpaper or fabric. With a little
patience, you can create something
totally unique.

It is probably easiest to begin
with some floral wallpaper.
Cut out the individual flowers and
arrange them as you will – possibly
in a tight posy, in a garland (which
could take a beautiful monogram in
the centre) or as a repeat pattern
with maybe three or five flowers
placed in a trellis outline. If the
desired effect is the flower bending
another way, simply trace it and
turn it over. (This might be useful
for balancing a group of flowers in a
basket). If the flowers need to be a
different size, photocopy the cut-out
and enlarge or reduce them by
various degrees, playing with them
until they look right. When you are
happy with the appearance, stick
them down with Spray-mount or
paper glue.

If you are copying a fabric, you
may wish to trace the flower and
leaf motifs rather than cut the cloth.
Proceed in the same way as for the
wallpaper. The only disadvantage
here is that your tracings will not
be coloured.

Floral runner

This attractive runner was originally used as a bell pull, a device used to summon servants in many of the grander British houses. The pull was linked – by a series of ingenious wires – to a bell in the servants' hall in a far-distant part of the house. There, each bell would be labelled with "Dining Room" or "Red Drawing Room" or

"Lady Anne's Chamber", etc. Most needlepoint bell pulls that survive today are from the 19th century. Whether this is because of some significant change in servant habits or whether it is purely that older examples have been destroyed by moths is not known. This piece is very old and is stitched in wool on particularly coarse canvas, with individual flowers and flower sprays mounted on a backing of silk. It is not clear whether the original canvas surrounding the flowers had rotted away, or whether it was always intended to work the flowers as "slips" and to cut them out and mount them on different fabric.

Looking closely at the flowers on the runner, you can see that the mesh of the different pieces of canvas does not always run in line with each other. For this reason, a template of the design has been provided (on the following pages, 102–105) showing the complete design. If you prefer, you can use just a section of it. It can be worked in tent stitch or any other decorative stitches you would like to include.

RIGHT AND ABOVE This runner was originally used as bell pull. Stitched in wool on a coarse canvas, individual flowers have been mounted on a backing of silk.

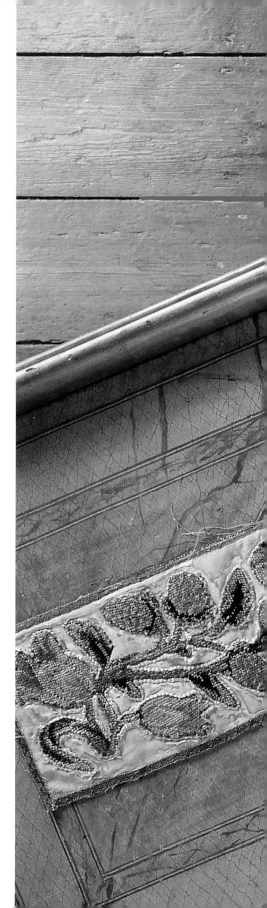

ABILITY LEVEL
Intermediate

FINISHED SIZE
Template is actual size

THREAD
Appleton's Crewel Wool

Colour	No
Sky blue	564
	567
Grey	883
Rose pink	754
Bright-rose pink	948
Coral	863
	865
Grey-green	351
Brown olive	311
	312
	313
Charcoal	998

NEEDLE SIZE   20

CANVAS   14-mesh

STITCHES   Tent

WORKING THE DESIGN
Follow the template provided here, using the colours listed above.

It is very helpful to colour this project first, whether you plan to work it in tent, long and short or any other stitch. For the tulip on this page: to gain definition (as you will be working over the outlines) you will need at least three shades of a colour – there is the petal that lies on top (usually the lightest shade), the two outside shades of the petals (medium shade) and the inside of the flower (darkest shade). By colouring with three crayons, you will see how the flower comes to life and assumes depth.

Romany rose tie-back

Tie-backs make all the difference to a pair of curtains. With natural cotton fabric like that making up these curtains, a bold pattern on a tie-back transforms them into a special window treatment. Tie-backs also drape open curtains in a much softer curve at the window and help gain extra light if they are over-full. If you have curtains made from a floral fabric, you could trace some of the flowers onto canvas and stitch them to match (see page 99).

Even though tie-backs are a comparatively small project, they need careful planning if they are to look attractive. The curtains here have only one fabric width in each side but they are interlined which adds to their bulk; curtains with more widths in each drop will need longer tie-backs. Before cutting canvas or planning any design, it is wise to experiment with a fabric offcut, or a length of lining fabric, to establish just what length the tie-back should be so that your curtains look their best.

The beauty of these individual flowers is that they can be spaced out along the length of each tie-back to suit your particular curtains. Remember to reverse the pattern for either side of the window so that you are working the deep-pink rose close to the end that will go at the back edge of the curtain.

If a group of flowers, or any motif, is stitched in the middle, it looks best when the whole design can be seen from the front, when facing the window. Use two hooks instead of one. Place the one that will take the front half of the tie-back further out on the window architrave, and the other behind the curtain but closer to the window pane so that the complete central motif is on view.

LEFT Tie-backs are a relatively simple piece of needlepoint to undertake, but they can make all the difference to a window treatment. These flowers, charted overleaf, can be spaced out along each tie-back to suit your particular curtains.

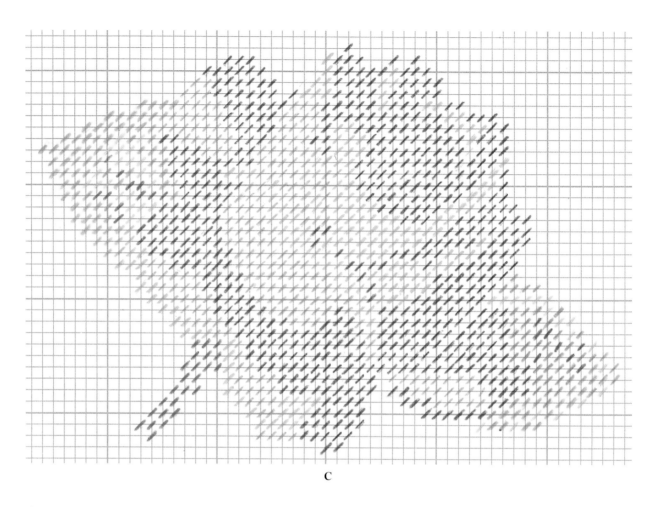

C

ABILITY LEVEL
Beginner

FINISHED SIZE
9 x 60cm/3½ x 24in

THREAD
Appleton's Crewel Wool

NEEDLE SIZE
20

CANVAS
14-mesh

STITCHES
Tent

WORKING THE DESIGN
Follow the chart and colours as
indicated.

ALTERNATIVE IDEAS
Another charming idea for holding
curtains back are fabric sashes which
could be decorated with needlepoint
slips. The sashes are long, narrow
strips of self-lined fabric, widening
out at both ends. The small
needlepoint design would be worked
as normal, trimmed and couched
onto one of the wide ends before it
was backed.

To be substantial, the fabric
chosen should be firmly-woven and
of sufficient weight to take the
canvas. All the edges of the trimmed
canvas can be edged with a
decorative couching similar to that
holding the flower garland in place
on the floral runner on page 100.

An alternative method would be to
use waste canvas. This is the canvas
that is mounted on a firm fabric,
the design stitched using the grid
of canvas threads for accuracy and
the canvas removed on completion,
leaving the design sitting on the
fabric. Waste canvas was another
Victorian fashion, and it is still
available today. I have also had
success with normal canvas,
providing that the design is not too

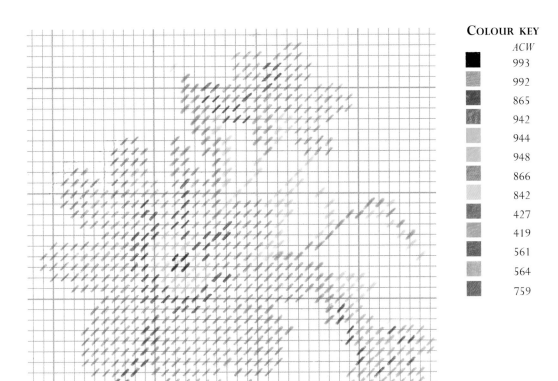

C

COLOUR KEY

ACW

■	993
■	992
■	865
■	942
■	944
■	948
■	866
■	842
■	427
■	419
■	561
■	564
■	759

dense. For example, the daisies on this page would be a better choice than the rose in the previous project.

TO WORK A PIECE

1 Choose firmly-woven fabric with minimum stretch. A worsted fabric would be good.

2 Position the canvas (only a little larger than the design you plan) on the ground fabric. Tack in place and mount both on the frame.

3 Stitch the design as usual.

4 With sharp-pointed scissors, cut the canvas midway between the motifs. Unravel the horizontal and vertical canvas threads.

5 With tweezers, gently pull out the canvas threads; by cutting midway between motifs you will have tails to grab with the tweezers.

REPEATING FLORAL PATTERNS

You may like to consider using just one floral motif as a repeating element in a larger design and need to have a mirror image. This bunch of daisies and other flowers would be a good example – it could look very fresh stitched on canvas in columns with alternate columns staggered in between and facing the other direction (what is known as a "half-drop" pattern repeat). To plot a mirror image, you can graph the design on grid paper using the same colours as the original chart here. Every time the stitches are shown to the left you will fill them in to the right. Alternatively, you can trace the original on tracing paper and then place the tracing paper either onto a light table or tape it to the window so that you are looking at the back. Now mark the stitches that you can see through, but make the diagonal of each stitch on the other angle.

Shell box-top

Panels for box lids have always been popular with needle-women. In fact, in times past, a box-top panel – especially when worked in needlepoint – appears to have been the culmination of a girl's training in stitchery.

The shell motif on this box (stitched using cross stitch, tent stitch and Victorian pattern darning) looks extremely modern, although it is actually part of a 19th-century design. Many woven fabrics, especially printed chintz, have a seaweed effect as a background. The original panel from which this design has been adapted, had three shells surrounded by a leafy border. It was believed to have been made in about 1830, when "seaweed" effects were extremely fashionable and appeared on woven shawls and in many textile pattern books.

Boxes can make good presents for both men and women. A small box like this can be used for storing everything from loose change, cuff links or other small personal treasures. A monogram or motif directly related to its contents or prospective owner could be worked, along with the same border and back-ground. If your box is a different shape or size, centre the motif and adapt the border to suit. For a larger box you should consider five rows of cross stitch rather than three (see chart on page 113).

Making up projects such as this is comparatively simple, as boxes can often be purchased with the four pieces of polished edging ready-mitred to fit the top. Instructions have been given on page 112 for the precise making-up procedure that should be followed.

LEFT Boxes make excellent gifts for everyone. This box-top features a shell design, but monograms or a motif related to its contents could also be worked, with the same border.

ABILITY LEVEL
Intermediate

FINISHED SIZE
19 x 12cm/7½ x 4⅛in

THREAD
Medici Wool Art 475 (25m/25¼yd skeins) & DMC Pearl Cotton no.5

MEDICI WOOL ART

Colour	No	Skeins
Navy	—	1
	8207	1
	8512	3*
	8104	2
	8176	1

DMC PEARL COTTON NO 5

	827	1
Ecru	—	1

* If a solid stitch such as diagonal/basketweave tent stitch is worked rather than one such as the Victorian pattern darning, as in the photograph, an extra skein may well be needed.

NEEDLE SIZE
20

CANVAS
14-mesh in brown

STITCHES
Cross, tent, Victorian pattern darning II

WORKING THE DESIGN
1 Find the middle of the canvas and mark with a small pencil cross. Mount on the frame.

2 Centre the shell on the canvas and work following chart 1 (opposite, above) and the colours indicated. The infill for the shell, which is left void on the chart, is worked in 8512 Medici wool.

3 Following chart 2 (opposite, below), work the three-row cross-stitch border. The background shown is Victorian pattern darning II (see page 21).

MAKING UP
4 Buy a ready-made box with four pieces of polished edging ready-mitred to fit the top.

5 When you have completed your piece of needlepoint, check carefully that it fits the dimensions of the box accurately. Trim any spare canvas to four threads from the finished stitching (although if your box has a wider wooden surround, you could leave a few more threads bordering on all sides).

6 Use a thin wadding/batting, interlining or dimette cut to the inside dimension of the box-top (subtracting the width of the wooden frame. Place that centrally, put the needlepoint on top and be sure to check that all the design will show when the frame is fixed.

7 The padding will have taken up the canvas, absorbing any unevenness in the back of the stitching. If the complete design does not fit perfectly, you can add another thin layer of padding.

8 Glue the four wooden frames over the unstitched area of canvas and then clamp until dry.

INITIALS AND MONOGRAMS
For initials or monograms, the waste canvas technique described on page 109 could be used.

COLOUR KEY

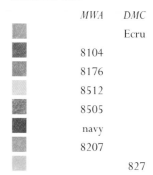

	MWA	DMC
		Ecru
	8104	
	8176	
	8512	
	8505	
	navy	
	8207	
		827

C

C

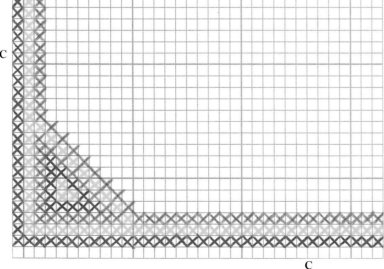

C

Sewing accessories

Needlework tools, and bags, boxes or caskets to keep them in, were a very important accessory for the elegant lady in the past. In "polite" society, this stitching was normally a frivolous or decorative piece. Public darning was not approved of.

To augment the elegant needlework, there were many attractive tools – pretty scissors, silver thimbles and elegant pincushions, for example. Indeed, antique needlework tools are both fascinating and beautiful.

To keep and protect the precious needle – and frequently even a large house would only have one – needlecases were made in the most exquisitely worked materials, including ivory, silver and mother-of-pearl. Nowadays, needlecases are more utilitarian, often in small book form like this one, with "pages" of flannel into which the needles can be inserted. It is popular to attach them to the end of a length of decorative ribbon (or possibly a narrow needlepoint band) with a pair of scissors to balance them at the other end, the whole thing to be worn around the neck to keep the items handy.

RIGHT AND ABOVE Needlework accessories, such as the needlecase and sewing bag shown here, were important accessories for the 18th- and 19th-century lady. They exemplify clever use of borders and motifs to create effective designs.

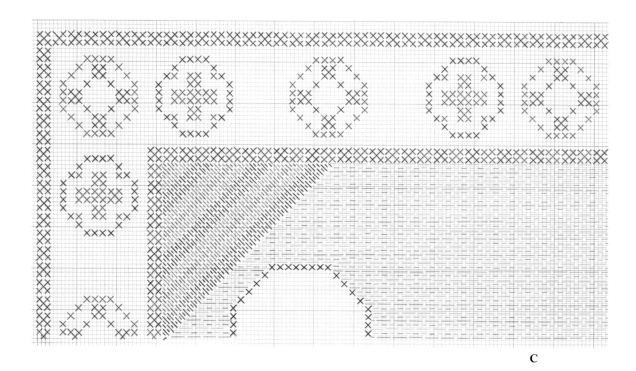

C

Colour key

ACW

▨	692
▨	693
▨	866
▨	327

Sewing Bag

ABILITY LEVEL
Intermediate

FINISHED SIZE
42 x 24cm/16½ x 9½in

THREAD/QUANTITIES
Appleton's Crewel Wool

Colour	No	Hanks
Honeysuckle	692	1
Honeysuckle	693	1½
Marine Blue	327	1
Coral	866	1

NEEDLE SIZE   20

CANVAS
16-mesh

STITCHES
Hungarian, Diagonal Florence, cross, tent, crossed corners

[NB. "C" denotes centre of chart. There is an overlap of 11 lines.]

WORKING THE DESIGN
1 Use 3-ply wool throughout.

2 Before mounting the canvas onto a frame, find the middle and, using an HB pencil, mark a large cross from the middle right out to the edges of the canvas.

3 Holding the canvas portrait-fashion, mark the word "TOP" on one short side.

4 Working from the middle, count sideways out in both directions 42 threads, then 4, 24, 4. Working up and down the canvas, count 100 threads in both directions, then 4, 24 and finally 4. This will give a central rectangle of 200 x 84 threads.

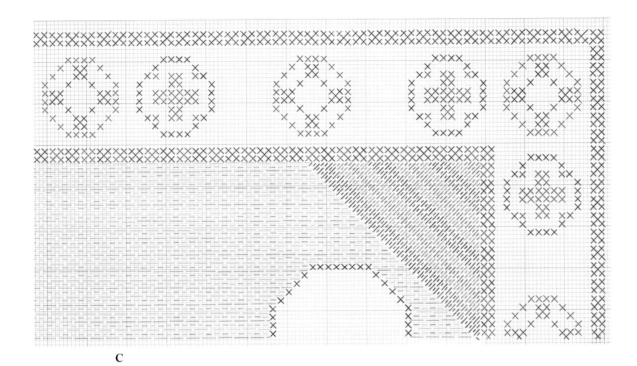

C

5 Work crossed corners stitch alternately in the blue 327 and coral 866, in the inner 4-thread channel.

6 Work the two large cross-stitch motifs inside this frame in blue 327.

7 Work the outer row of crossed corners in blue 327 in the other four-thread channel.

8 Following the charts provided here, work the small cross-stitch motifs in the border area, spaced as shown, with the infills of crossed corners and cross stitch as shown.

9 Work diagonal Florence (see page 23 in *Before You Begin* section) as shown on the chart, starting with two rows of blue 327 in the centre-bottom. The colour order is as shown: two rows blue 327, one row honeysuckle 693, one row coral 866, one row 693, two rows 327, etc.

10 Now work Hungarian stitch in horizontal rows in the two shades of honeysuckle. Start the first stitch over 4 threads in the centre-bottom, sharing with the blue diagonal Florence as shown on the chart.

11 Work the basketweave tent stitch both inside the large cross-stitch motifs and in the border behind and between the small cross-stitch motifs.

MAKING UP

The simplest way to make up this sewing bag is to stretch it as usual and line it by slipstitching a lining (a closely-woven rayon dress lining would be suitable).

If preferred, it could be made up in the style of a sewing roll or *hussif*.

A *hussif,* or "housewife", contains all the basic necessities for sewing and mending. A very plain version was issued to all soldiers and sailors in Britain, although the far more glamorous design shown here is well work the extra effort.

Stretch as usual, and then make up a lining panel with a narrow strip of fabric sewn on in a series of loops (to take individual skeins of stranded cotton etc.), and a panel of flannel to take needles. Slipstitch this completed panel to the back of the needlepoint. Fill with your needlepoint necessities and enjoy.

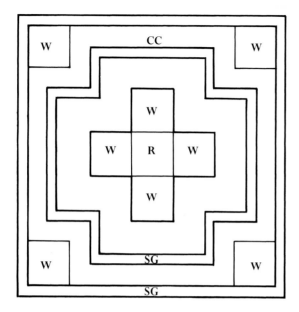

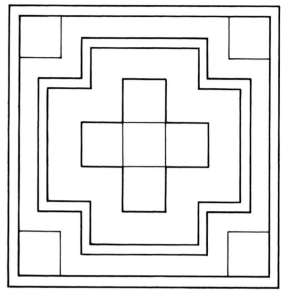

Needlecase

The front and back of this needlecase has a central panel of diagonal tartan which is also used behind the oak leaves on the Tartan rug (see page 78). Small items such as this look particularly effective worked in pearl cotton, skeins of which given below.

ABILITY LEVEL Intermediate

FINISHED SIZE
15.5 x 7.5cm/6 x 3in, folded to give a 7.5 x 7.5cm/3 x 3in booklet

STITCHES
Waffle, crossed corners, diagonal tartan, sloping gobelin, rhodes

THREAD/QUANTITIES
DMC Pearl Cotton no. 5 & DMC Stranded Cotton

DMC PEARL COTTON

Colour	No	Skeins
Ecru	—	½
Navy	3750	1

DMC STRANDED COTTON

Rose pink	223	2

NEEDLE SIZE
22

CANVAS
18-mesh

WORKING THE DESIGN
1 Holding the canvas landscape fashion, follow the "road map" of the design provided above.

W is the position for a waffle stitch
R is the position for a rhodes stitch
SG is for sloping gobelin.

2 Work the stitches in the following colours: waffle stitches (see page 22 in *Before You Begin*) should be worked in the rose 223 stranded cotton; the rhodes stitches (see page 22) are in 3750 pearl cotton, the first two stitches of the crossed corners are worked in 223 and the tipping stitches are worked in ecru pearl cotton.

3 Next, work the sloping gobelin in navy 3750. Alter the angle of the stitch in the centre of each side.

4 Work diagonal tartan, following the instructions on page 22.

RECIPE
2 rows rose pink 223
4 rows ecru
2 rows navy 3750
4 rows ecru

[As always, work the AB position completely, quarter-turn the canvas and repeat the same recipe.]

TO MAKE UP
1 When the work has been completed, take the canvas off the frame, fold along the spine of the case (where there are still 4 threads bare) and work long-legged cross stitch with navy 3750, aligning the canvas threads, stitching as one layer.

2 Trim excess canvas to 6 threads on all sides, finger press and hem them to the back of the work. Then slipstitch a lining fabric to the piece.

3 Cut out 2 pieces of felt or wool (this will prevent pins and needles from rusting) to make four "pages" which will take the needles.

4 Backstitch the pages in place down the centre, taking care to stitch through to the back of the canvas and not just through the lining. In the model, a felt that matched one of the coloured threads was used for both the lining and the pages, but cream would also look good.

NEEDLEWORK ACCESSORIES

From earliest times, needlework tools, and the caskets to keep them in, had both a practical and a decorative purpose; they were frequently made out of semi- or even precious materials, and looked very attractive.

In 18th-century England, and slightly later in the United States, fancy needlework and its accessories became viewed as ornaments for the fashionable lady. A woman of means would spend a large proportion of her time visiting her women friends during the day and attending dinners and balls in the evening.

There had always been essential tools, spinning wheels, looms, yarn winders and clamps in even simple homes and women enjoyed stitching in company. Reputedly, Mary Queen of Scots spent most of her time in captivity at Hardwick Hall, England, stitching with her ladies. Meanwhile, "sewing bees" were popular parties in America where the early settlers had to salvage and re-use every piece of fabric that they could.

COLOUR KEY

DMC

Ecru (pearl)

223 (stranded)

3750 (pearl)

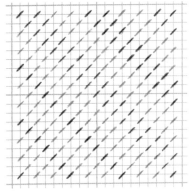

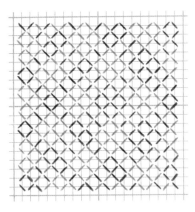

Daisy purse

The central feature of this pretty purse is a stylized design of blue flowers. This would make an excellent repeat pattern for many different types of needlepoint projects.

The rose sprigs around the border are deceptively complex as, even in the area shown in the photograph, there are five different sprigs. However, they are quite restrained, and you may prefer to employ a stronger border for the blue flowers and keep this more delicate border for something else.

This pattern also comes from the Mary Dowell Pattern Piece (see page 30). The blue flowers were stitched as they appear here, but the rose sprigs were stitched in cream on a burgundy background. These motifs appear quite early on the Pattern Piece and if, as it would appear, Mrs Dowell joined the individual pieces in approximate date order, they would have been made in about 1840–45.

The patterns were probably published in a ladies' journal of the period. Magazines or journals, such as *The Lady's Magazine* with the subtitle of an "entertaining companion for the fair sex", were published in the late 18th century in England. A similar American publication was called *Godey's Lady's Book* (1830–98). While they contained excellent designs for embroidered accessories of all types, most copies seen today do not have any of the designs intact. They have been torn out and used for pricking the pattern onto the fabric. In the mid-19th century, it was commonplace for magazines to have a "free" pattern included, but it was not bound in – so these loose sheets have usually not survived.

LEFT The stylized blue flowers and the rose sprig border of this purse is another pattern from the Mary Dowell sampler. If you wish, you can use a stronger border than the quite restrained one here.

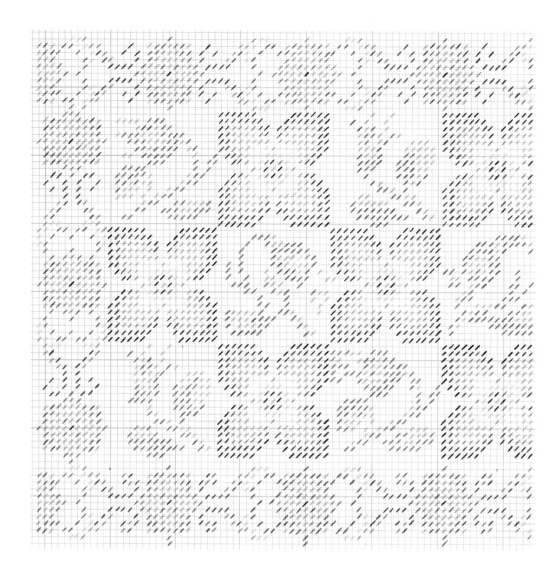

ABILITY LEVEL
Easy

FINISHED SIZE
23 x 11.5cm/9 x 4⅝in

THREAD
Appleton's Crewel Wool

NEEDLE SIZE 20

CANVAS
14-mesh

STITCHES
Tent

WORKING THE DESIGN
Follow the chart and colours indicated. (5 line overlap each side.)

TO MAKE UP
This useful little purse could be used for many different things – it could, for example, be used as a practical case for holding writing materials, sewing equipment, make-up/cosmetics or money. Stretch and line the canvas as usual, choosing the lining fabric according to the end purpose – ie. waterproof fabric would be sensible choice for a make-up bag.

Fold the piece in half and, using binding stitch (see page 21 in *Before You Begin*), stitch the two ends together with the deep blue wool. A zip could be added as a way of closing the top opening.

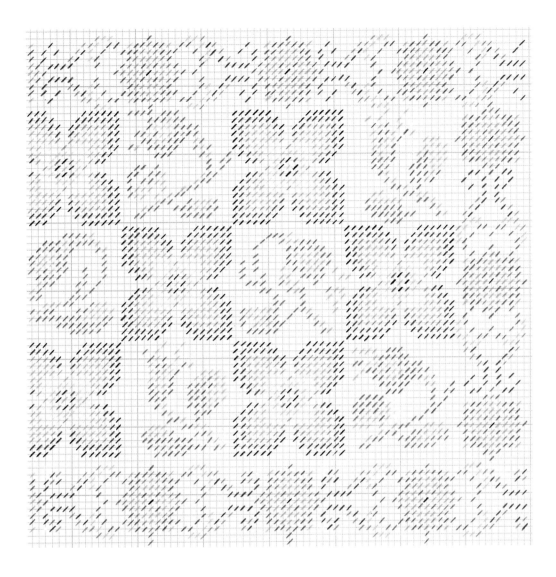

COLOUR KEY

	ACW			ACW
■	993			242
	992			747
	947			472
	755		■	568
	753			563
	245			561
	243			

Index

Acknowledgements

Many thanks to the Strangers Hall Museum, Norwich, and in particular Cathy Terry, for allowing us to photograph the Victorian chair, the Parterre cushion, the small purse and to adapt the Shell Box top from a larger piece; to Norah Tuck, the owner of the Mary Dowell Pattern Piece; to the Earl and Countess of Harewood for permission to make the miniature rug from the carpet in their house; to Alistair Sampson Antiques of Mount Street, London, for allowing us to photograph both the Tiger Rug and the Delft picture.

Thank you also to Sara Stonor who, besides always being there at moments of panic, made up all the new projects quite beautifully; Pamela Clabburn who helped with dating some of the pieces and who has always been an inspiration; to Philipe Cecile for enlightening me about the Victorian chaise de voyeuse; and the Orford Gallery, Norwich who framed the Berlin woolwork charts and the bead picture. Thanks also to Chapel Yard for supplying flowers and accessories; to Nice Irma's, Jane Turner Upholstery, The Natural Fabric Company, VV Rouleaux, Elm Hill Crafts and to Pat Cutforth.

To Helena and Raymond Turvey for their excellent charts; Margot Richardson for being such a calm editor; Deena Beverley and Tim Imrie for the lovely photographs; everyone at Mitchell Beazley; and my agent Fiona Lindsay.

Thanks to my husband Patrick who, besides all else, checked colours; to Melinda Brown who kept the rest of the studio under control while I stitched and wrote; and finally to Joy who kept everyone supplied with coffee!

Anna Pearson, 1996

Some of the designs in this book are available as complete kits. Write for details to: Pearson Design, Keswick Mill, Norwich, Norfolk, England.